792·8 ROY

D1465245

DRAMATIC DANCE

Coleg Sir Gâr
Canolfan Dysgu
Llanelli
Learning Centre

DRAMATIC DANCE

An Actor's Approach to Dance as a Dramatic Art

DARREN ROYSTON

B L O O M S B U R Y

LONDON • NEW DELHI • NEW YORK • SYDNEY

Bloomsbury Methuen Drama

An imprint of Bloomsbury Publishing Plc

50 Bedford Square	1385 Broadway
London	New York
WC1B 3DP	NY 10018
UK	USA

www.bloomsbury.com

Bloomsbury is a registered trademark of Bloomsbury Publishing Plc

First published 2014

© Darren Royston, 2014

All rights reserved. No part of this publication may be reproduced or transmitted in any form or by any means, electronic or mechanical, including photocopying, recording, or any information storage or retrieval system, without prior permission in writing from the publishers.

Darren Royston has asserted his right under the Copyright, Designs and Patents Act, 1988, to be identified as author of this work.

No responsibility for loss caused to any individual or organization acting on or refraining from action as a result of the material in this publication can be accepted by Bloomsbury or the author.

British Library Cataloguing-in-Publication Data
A catalogue record for this book is available from the British Library.

ISBN: PB: 978-1-4081-7381-7
ePDF: 978-1-7809-3314-6
ePub: 978-1-7809-3315-3

Library of Congress Cataloging-in-Publication Data
Royston, Darren.
Dramatic dance: an actor's approach to dance as a dramatic art / Darren Royston.
pages cm
Includes bibliographical references and index.
ISBN 978-1-4081-7381-7 (pbk.)– ISBN 978-1-78093-314-6 (web-ready pdf)– ISBN 978-1-78093-315-3 (ebook) 1. Dance–Psychological aspects. 2. Drama. 3. Movement (Acting) I. Title.
GV1588.5.R68 2014
792.8–dc23
2013036374

Typeset by Fakenham Prepress Solutions, Fakenham, Norfolk NR21 8NN
Printed and bound in India

To all the dancing satyrs who follow Dionysos

and the snail shells that remain

CONTENTS

INTRODUCTION: ALTERNATIVE APPROACHES – MAKING DANCE DRAMATIC

At the beginning of every new course I teach at RADA, I always begin by saying:

> On the timetable it says you will now receive a dance class …
> Well, actually we will not be teaching you how to dance.
> You are not here to become dancers, but to develop as actors.
> You have joined an academy for dramatic art.
> So, instead, you will learn how you can use dance as a dramatic art.

This distinction is very important to me. It means that the actors will be able to use whatever previous training or experience of dance they already possess. It does not mean that they will not gain new skills and develop useful and practical techniques in dance, but the reason for learning dance as a dramatic art is very specific.

Dance is part of the art of theatre. Dance cannot exist on its own in the context of dramatic performance. It connects movement with communication, improvisation and performance. Dance works in conjunction with other elements to enable meanings to be created in performance. For actors to perform dance as part of the drama, they must master the art of dance in this particular context. This book offers several approaches which can contribute to developing this understanding and training this skill. The aim is that the whole active and thinking body and mind are fully engaged with the task of making dance an integral and vital part of theatre.

You will notice straight away that each chapter in this book has a title that locates the material to a specific era and time period. However, this is not a textbook on the history of dance, as such. Dance history is being used to give an imaginative context for the activity of dance. This historical evidence should be used to inspire feelings in the actor that can then be expressed through performance in the present moment. There is a need to generalize and to categorize the material into a particular 'period' so that, sometimes, we give the abbreviation 'period dance' to the classes on the drama school timetable. So, for this book, I have selected some ideas and dance forms from a selection of time periods that can also develop a way of making dance performance dramatic.

Part of the approach in this book is how the body can adapt to display different styles. Specific historical dances will be used to demonstrate how variations exist between different societies. A specific historical period may be represented by the style of dancing performed by that particular society. Certain dancing techniques may be identified with these historical circumstances. However, a lot of these skills will also be transferable between the different time periods. Various approaches will train the actor to use these dances in a dramatic way, so I have chosen certain elements from the body of historical material that can inspire actors to move confidently, and have fun with the lessons.

Sometimes people mock the subject, dubbing 'historical dance' with the title '*histerical* dance'. That never worries me as a teacher, as I firmly believe that if the students are finding enjoyment in the material they will also get a sense of why this strange activity of moving in what is now a 'weird way' might have been entertaining for the people living at the time. It is strange to imagine that we ourselves would have behaved differently if we had lived in another time period, so the aim for the actor is to discover how a true feeling can be expressed through different artistic forms that may differ from now. We laugh at a fashion when it is no longer in vogue, but we need to imagine what it felt to wear this outfit when it was the norm, and the people wearing this fashion felt 'cool'.

The chapters will include some suggestions for more serious historical research that could be followed up: for example, original sources and academic commentary on this evidence that could be studied, as well as suggestions of things in other disciplines that might help an actor place the material into a bigger picture – quite literally. What art relates to the period? What music was being played? Who lived at this time that may have spent time doing these dances? Now that we can search things very quickly on the internet, the decision has been made to give keywords in the text which can send you into the right direction to find out more and begin your own independent research.

The question remains the same for each chapter, in whatever era or time period. Why are people moving in this dance dimension? Believable answers can only by found when the body turns the imagination into physical action. Each chapter will produce its own recipe to produce the particular physical result, with the hope that this will also inspire personal responses, alternative exercises and imagined situations, rather than simply present a step-by-step syllabus. However, there are certain approaches which will always be found in play, so this introduction will now explain the philosophy that supports the idea that dance can be performed as a dramatic art.

The Actor Approach to Dance

The main question for this book is: how can the dances of history become dramatic dance?

Time Travel to the Dance Dimension

As you begin a new chapter, I invite you to imagine you are being transported to a different historical world. Each chapter gives a brief introduction to the particular style of the particular dance world you are about to enter.

An Actor Prepares to …

As an actor, you must be prepared to dance, so the body needs to be warmed up to be ready to take on very specific instructions for moving parts of the body, responding freely to music and imaginative exercises, and being receptive to others in the studio. Each chapter gives some exercises that will gradually warm the body up, while also getting the mind thinking about the reality of the world where the dance was a current activity.

Setting the Scene

- What are the educational, scientific and cultural reasons for considering this time period as important, and which section of society is dancing in this world?
- What elements do those joining the dance share?
- How do these ideas translate physically?
- What terminology is used to communicate dance instructions in practice?
- How can this physical activity of understanding what makes up a dance form be useful for the actor as an artist?

Every dance exists in a context of given circumstances as much as a scene of dialogue and action; there is purpose and intention in steps and movements in the same way that actors may consider objectives and actions in the preparation of a scene.

Four Practical Approaches

The book presents four practical approaches on each topic. These four approaches can be considered separately, but you will find they overlap and combine in practice. I have called them:

Expressive Dance, Historical Dance, Laban Dance and Show Dance.

You may decide to give them your own names, deciding which is most appropriate at different times: in actor training, in preparation for a role, in creating dances and scenes with dance, exploring the period of the play during rehearsal and learning a technique for dancing in the performance of drama. In some ways, each approach is saying the same thing in its own way, with the aim of combining thought with action. Each chapter will prioritize different approaches, as the most relevant for an actor using the material in a practical way.

I have chosen to find sound-bite titles within the chapters, which suggest something about the nature of each exercise. These are not intended to belittle the importance of the techniques developed over time, but to try to get you to jump in at the deep end quickly and start doing the exercise rather than trying to explain everything beforehand. The aim is to allow you to make connections with your own experience in dance, theatre and life, so that the exercise is a personal expression. Don't try to be someone from another period – just put yourself physically in each differently constructed world.

Here is a description of each category with the explanation of how it is a different approach to the same theme.

Expressive Dance

What abstract themes are being expressed and how can this expression create a 'movement mode'?

This is dancing as a chance for free expression and exploration. It is part of the process to lose inhibitions and start moving in ways different from daily life. The 'dance dimension' is to be considered a place for open interaction and improvisation. Through movement exercises based on the theme, you will be asked to draw on your past experiences, remembered images and personal thoughts and feelings. Every interpretation is right if the actor feels it expresses the theme for them, with their full moving bodies combining with their concentrated focused minds. This should always be a good warm-up, requiring the whole body to be moving around the studio. Ideas will be explored freely, so that there is no right or wrong at this stage, as long as the actor is engaged with the ideas while moving the whole body. The themes should be used as ways to approach movement exercises – as games to play with – which may produce ways of moving that make the ideas visible in the studio. The outcome is the creation of a 'movement mode' by which I mean a way of moving that everyone in the studio creates together, sharing in the experience. Interaction with other moving bodies then can establish how the particular movement style was shared in a society at a moment in history. Abstract ideas and representation in art can inspire this approach.

Historical Dance

What specific elements from the historical context can be emphasized in performance and how is this way of moving particular to a moment in time?

This is dancing with the knowledge of history. Historical dances are dead, buried, probably forgotten, and therefore can only be revived actively, by the actor using an active historical imagination. Consider the people and the place. How was the dance floor a place of negotiation and establishment; for instance, relating to the social, political and sexual negotiations particular to that society, and the creation of status and hierarchy to maintain the order of this society? From where did it come? How did people of a past period create these dances? How did the social rules create movement modes, manners, etiquette and recognized style identifiers? What links can be made to the music, visual arts and cultural developments of this historical period, and was an artistic aesthetic established alongside? How can an actor use historical evidence to create a physical performance: such as dance instruction manuals, guides to polite conduct and historical choreography deciphered from descriptions and notations? Practical exercises based on this research connects a particular physical technique to a way of moving, creating an awareness of the historical body.

The chapters in this book follow a basic chronological structure. If you follow the chapters in order, you will move, quite literally, through a historical development from the classical worlds to the beginning of the twentieth century. Certain evidence from each chapter will be more useful in practice for an actor working on a role set at this particular time period. It may be useful to also consider the original practice of the actors when working on classical texts with references that will need to be researched and reinterpreted in modern theatre or film performance. To remain aware of the various styles from the different periods, you will need to have an analytical approach to your movement study.

Laban Dance

What technical skills can be used to give the illusion that the performing body belongs to the imagined world and how is this shared as a dynamic experience?

This book considers an analytical approach to the discipline and art of dance. It is influenced by the principles of dance and the art of movement as systematized by Rudolf Laban and used with all types of movement study, including being developed with the actor, dancer, choreographer and performance artist in mind.

Rudolf Laban (1879–1958) was a pioneer of dance and movement study in the twentieth century, who worked with many individuals, in many countries. His work has influenced many teachers of dance and acting, and this developed work has become part of many programmes of actor training. Throughout his life, Laban himself continued to explore movement as an art, and was influenced at different times by a diverse range of disciplines, philosophies and cultures including the Dada Cabaret, Karl Gustav Jung psychoanalysis, Contemporary Dance and Austruckdanz Dance Theatre. His work specifically applied to actor training was professionally promoted by Jean Newlove (movement director to Joan Littlewood's Theatre Workshop) and in theatre choreography by Geraldine Stephenson (who also developed work in historical dance for film and TV). Now, Laban's work is best known in the Eight Action Efforts, sometimes abbreviated to 'The Efforts'.

This book will also draw upon other elements of Laban's work that can be used by actors to consider dance as a dramatic art, particularly with the use of rhythms in space and time. These elements have been given different names through history: Space Harmony (Choreutics), Movement Dynamics (Eukinetics), Choreosophy (Wisdom of Circles), Tanz-Ton-Wort (Dance-Sound-Word Triad), Architectonics and Spatial Scaffolding, Swinging Scales of Movement, Laban Movement Analysis, Choreology and Choreological Studies, Posture Gesture Merger and Movement Profiling. Using symbols to record movement was proposed as a way to write down movement, to generate something akin to a score as used in music, and this system has developed into Labanotation or Kinetography Laban. Laban included dance exercises in his early writings, such as the *Manuals for Gymnastic Training* (1923) and *Choreography* (1926), which suggested themes and styles that could develop a systematic approach when training physically. Established dance forms and historical material could be examined using the Laban Approach to consider how the meaning was conveyed through particular movement codes. The main written text by Laban with a focus on drama is *The Mastery of Movement for the Stage* (1951). Here, Laban writes that the aim of the actor must be to be able to 'think in terms of movement'. The technical analysis and the discipline of this approach strives to attain this vital skill.

In this book, each chapter will consider how 'thinking in terms of movement' may help us understand how the body is working technically as an organism in the space, and how we can sense a particular way of moving as both an actor and as a member of the audience. This role of the 'onlooker' may be someone who would have witnessed the dance in its original social context (such as a member of the same society), or someone who watched a contemporary depiction of the dance in a theatrical event (the historical audience), or someone engaging with the performance in the present day (an audience now). This Laban Dance movement analysis will see how different layers may interact and combine. A 'body language' is something that is created in practice, and may change in different cultures, so from this analytical standpoint, the way that dance can be performed by an actor today will become the most important thing. Each actor needs to consider what the audience will be aware of during dance performance today.

Show Dance

What does the performer present to the audience and how does the audience participate in this performance?

This is dancing with the awareness of an audience. Exercises are all well and good, but how do you take these into performance? We need to consider how performance practice has changed and how audiences will view the dance. What resonances will the movement have today? How should a dance be choreographed, and what needs to be contained in a choreography, a dance scene or a routine? An actor may consider specific characters and how they might move, or scenes where dance occurs. An actor, director or choreographer will need to consider how the work explored in the studio, including the imaginative exploration, historical research and technical reconstructions, will need to be represented in a performance context.

Combining the Approaches

In summary, this book proposes a way for the performance of Dramatic Dance to combine practical knowledge from many different approaches.

For those using this book to create teaching plans, the four approaches can be combined in any order to give a methodical and creative structure. Exercises can be selected from each category, to make a structure moving from playful theme-based games (Expressive Dance), to thinking about the historical authenticity (Historical Dance), then considering the technical elements which are particular to this specific style (Laban Dance), and then taking elements of this material into consideration of performance for the audience today (Show Dance).

Depending on the available time, teachers may choose to spend an entire lesson on one section from a relevant category, or maybe spend a term in one historical period. The book can be used as a good follow-up for students who can then reconsider after class what has been done physically in one session, and make connections to further research, and find other resources by following links from the references.

Date Order

The chapters have been ordered with an historical chronological development, based on standard divisions in cultural periods, mainly with reference to Western European history. These themes connect very easily to Western classical theatre, from the Ancient Greeks, through Shakespeare and Restoration Comedy, to Victorian and twentieth-century period drama and beyond. Historical periods may of course be referred to in other imaginative ways, either as complete production interpretations or as a choice for an actor's role. It would be a hugely simplistic view to think that each historical period moved easily into the next, although I have found that teaching in sequence is very rewarding, as the students can order the material to match a time frame. I have therefore developed themes to suit the development of the actor's technique as a dancer. These follow a sequence moving from general to specific, as we travel forward in time from ancient to modern.

There is at least one benefit of beginning with early historical periods – we start at a point of relative ignorance! Dance historians have very few definite facts about these lost ancient cultures. Because of this, the actors are required to engage their imaginations immediately, rather than feel they have to revive a dead dance as an exact scientific task. Attention to detail is always important, but this is very different from having pressure to present historical authenticity. Having said all that, I have also taught separate workshops on isolated historical periods, and when working as a choreographer it may be that a particular production requires instruction on a particular dance or movement style: in this case it may be possible to select the relevant section.

My advice is that you should follow the lead of the dancing bodies and, as an actor, your own moving body. Whatever starts to produce the dramatic effect in the studio should be allowed to generate the process. When the feeling you are hoping to achieve with the dance starts to take shape, then let the dance become part of the drama. The most spontaneous and seemingly unrelated choices made while in the flow of dance creation can be the most revealing about the dramatic tension and can generate the dynamic of a good performance. Systematic analysis and repetition (that being the real meaning of rehearsal, of course) can then make sure the experience is channelled into memory. Memory was the mother of Terpsichore, the Greek muse of Dance, so it is a skill that is also needed for a competent performance. Using different approaches will make things easier to remember, using different ways of engaging with the desired quality.

Words of Warning

Only by doing can you understand dance. So use this book as a springboard to dance, not as a textbook to memorize by rote or follow word for word.

This book considers what must be avoided when executing a particular style. Confidence in a particular way of moving may mean that certain things become overstated, or develop beyond what is required. The actor may perform the move perfectly in the class, having worked through the exercises, but this moment needs to be *remembered* (meaning re-embodied) when it appears in performance, in the context of a scene in the play. The real reason for moving in that particular way may be forgotten and bad habits may creep in, so you are encouraged to use a combination of different approaches to keep the material alive for you, as a dancing actor.

Online Teaching Tools

Nonsuch Dance Reconstructions

In this book, I will refer to various sources that connect to the material, sometimes literally and sometimes not. Artists depict dance in each period, but even these visual references are not necessarily physically accurate. However, I recommend a number of online supporting materials. As far as possible, all references in the book are freely available through WIKIMEDIA COMMONS or equivalents. However, these are not prescriptive and you should enjoy discovering additional materials as part of the process of creating a context for your dramatic dance.

This book refers to online Nonsuch Dance Reconstuctions. You will find links to filmed footage of these reconstructions on p. 155. These are technical reconstructions of authentic dances for illustrative purposes. The music and choreographies are selected from teaching-aid manuals produced by Nonsuch History and Dance (a registered charity). They offer an extensive collection of dances from all periods of history, in replicated historical costumes and with appropriate music.

The Nonsuch Dance Reconstructions are performed out of context, and are not to be viewed as definitive models of dramatic dance. You are encouraged to consider the reconstructions and then respond creatively with a greater degree of confidence in the historical dance vocabulary. You yourself need to then make your own choices within the exercises and in the way you decide to act through the material. Notes in the chapters will explain how and why certain choices have been made, considering connections between the physical realization and the historical evidence. As an actor, you should be able to justify your performance according to its dramatic purpose.

Choreo-Captions

The Nonsuch Dance Reconstructions include captions. Sometimes these are abbreviations of technical terms that point to specific elements in this book that are drawn from historical dance manuals. For example, steps that repeat are shortened to their first letter (e.g. a Reverence – the technical term for a bow to your partner – appears as [R]). They should make it easier for you to consider what elements have been combined to create the dance structure. As in studying music, there is a need to know that the piece of music is created from individual sounding notes and rhythmical units, but then entire phrases need to be felt as being the creation of the composition as a whole. The micro-elements of the steps are then put into a macro-structure which, in the end, must be seen as simply 'the dance' – just as in performance the lines of the character will in the end be considered as 'the play'.

To move to this holistic performance, some of the captions will use sub-headings to identify sections within the dance. While most of these *choreo-captions* connect to traditional ways of determining new sections of dance by the spatial patterns made by the moving bodies (e.g. 'separating out'), these are only basic technical suggestions to get you to independently produce a more creative response to the shaping of the dance. I would suggest that students and teachers differentiate each section by finding names for the sections themselves.

You are encouraged to come up with your own *choreo-captions* that match how you yourself interpret each section of the dance, and connect to how it makes you perform this differently from other parts of the dance. The choreographies of each chapter are often comprised of very similar steps, so it is possible that by making each dance personal to you it can lessen the confusion between the different dances you learn. This process of captioning sections can be used as way to prevent you getting swamped by the mass of material as you experience many dances. Hopefully you will develop an historical framework for the dances and the movement styles attributed to different histories, and all the while link this to your muscle memory. So, to begin with, you may even want to connect to very specific things that happen in your studio and rehearsal situation – giving *choreo-caption* names to dance steps because of where you go in the studio ('the escape to the window') or relating to the narrative of the drama (e.g. 'the near-miss kiss' as you pass someone during a country dance), or the relationship between the characters' dancing and their intention.

When creating your own *choreo-captions*, it is of course good practice to try to connect to ideas that might have meant something to the people living at the time when the dance was in vogue, and to images that relate to the mood being evoked by the particular art of the dance. In other words, try not to be too anachronistic with your images – or do so with complete tongue-in-cheek awareness. For example, the word 'aeroplane arms' may be very acceptable with the swinging from side to side of the arms during the Charleston heel kicks, as the move may indeed have been feasibly inspired by the invention of the first aeroplanes in the earlier decades. However, when a similar placement of the arms occurs momentarily during the preparation for the two-hand-hold in the eighteenth-century minuet, it may not quite be appropriate to replicate two aeroplanes about to collide, since an eighteenth-century couple would have no idea what you were referring to. It may be better to title this move after the swooping of an eagle, for example, to still get the idea of gliding, while keeping the image connected to ideas the people of the time may have understood.

Above all though, I do encourage you to have fun choosing different names for parts of the dance, as this process of creatively renaming technical dance steps does allow you to engage imaginatively to the material, and think how the movement can be connected to meaning and communication as an actor.

Technical Terms

One other note needs to be made about the technical names for dance steps. The same dance term sometimes has a different meaning in a different historical period. The dance term will usually only be describing one element that is part of the execution of the step. Even when the dance term's meaning is deciphered, it may alter in a different context. For instance, the word *saltarelli* appears a number of times with different dances, and looks like a different way of moving in space with different steps. Some of these dances are even in the same collection of notated dances, but require a different interpretation by the dancing bodies to fit the choreography with the music and the space. It may be the exact technical phrase used in the original manuscript descriptions of these dances, but how it will look to someone watching will depend on other elements surrounding the dance: the musical structure, the spatial distance, the reason the person executes this step at this exact moment in the dance.

It is useful to be aware of the precise terminology in existence, but this book is also about processing this researched material into a physical approach that can allow the actor to explore and present different dance styles. For this reason, this book uses a methodology based on the Laban Dance analysis, with some concepts which can apply generally to dance as an art and adapted to the particular historical period. The historical context may alter how the same term is physicalized, so use this approach to understand the differences through the analysis of the movement in its own terms, and create categories that you yourself can differentiate.

The Context of Space: Visual Representation

Floor tracks will always be adapted for the location in which the dance is being performed. It must be remembered that the floor track is part of the dramatic language of the dance. Not only does this relate to how it feels to perform the dance in a particular location, and for a particular occasion, but also to the people who watch this particular dance as spectators. These elements need to be kept in mind when viewing the filmed dance reconstructions. The samples were filmed in one studio, with a combi-nation of different camera angles selected to help the viewer consider the three-dimensional element of the material. The positioning of the audience will play a part in how the dance is viewed and how this communicates the drama of a scene and the characters involved. Historical dance choreographies made for the royal courts of Europe consciously direct their live performance art to where the person with highest status is seated. The architecture of the room where the dance was being performed may have determined certain choices of where to move. This book considers evidence of such elements.

It is important to consider where the historical dance may have been performed when it was first living, that is to say, in its first physical existence. However, by undertaking this activity of making dramatic dance, I believe it is possible that the feeling of the historical dance can be rediscovered by the actors in a 'neutral' space, such as in a dance or drama studio. Imagination will be employed to think of the space where the historical dance would have been located. The filming of these samples is to assist the physical understanding of all the parts of the dance.

After this, it will necessary to consider the performance space where the dance is being presented: this is the Show Dance element of the book. This may be a theatrical environment, where the audience of spectators may require the choreographer to alter the dance to ensure it works within that set-up of audience and performers. The set design and the theatrical space will also add different layers of spatial perception that will need to be considered. The position of an audience external to the dance is a theatrical construction of space, so you will need to consider to which audience you are performing. Even if the dance were used in film, then the positioning of the camera would also play a major part in how the dramatic meaning of the dance is conveyed.

Historical Clothing

A certain style and fashion will influence a way of moving; however, it is also useful to note that the clothes may be chosen to emphasize an already established way of presenting the body. Each period will have different reasons for its particular fashion. The choice of clothing will be a part of the aesthetics and the theatre semiotics created in the performance mode, so wearing something as neutral as possible is encouraged for actors in training, before this decision has been made. If a selection of shoes and clothing are available to help understand the way the body may have felt at a particular time in history, then why not consciously wear the garment and step inside? The feeling from this experience should belong to your understanding of a physical state of being, and not only relate to a way of looking or dressing. You must not rely on wearing such items of clothing to find the feeling. The experience needs to be part of the muscular memory of the physical actor, to be connected with whenever needed.

Further Research Springboards

Each chapter concludes with a few suggestions of texts, images and music to be considered in a practical way. You are encouraged to research costume, décor, architecture, props and accessories, and any other material that will provide an overall picture of the period and the historical world you are imagining to be moving within. Each period could expand into many different areas – so I suggest whatever element interests you personally as an actor should be followed up, be it fashion or architecture or music or other cultural elements, and then this independent research can be shared and discussed with the group. It is always worth sharing ideas with the group you are working with, and then you can make links between the different material.

It is important to absorb the fact that creative research of this nature is rarely literal, and, especially within this area, the sources that do exist require interpretation in a delicate balance of understanding and informed imagination. Visual references may give you a feel for a period or for a dance, but should not be viewed as an illustration that you should act out precisely. The act of dancing has been depicted in art, but sometimes what is painted contradicts the documentary evidence, or is physically impossible to achieve in practice. Modern music may serve a purpose, especially where no existing music from the period can be located. Abstract artwork may provide clarity for abstract ideas. As an actor, you have to find connections to a range of materials that allow your own research join with the dance of *then* to become dramatic *now*, so you can be fully present in its action.

Historical dances are also frequently performed as part of theatre and film performance. It is worth considering how choreographers have adapted the historical material to satisfy the function of the dance in its particular dramatic context. Some productions may wish to simply convey an historical flavour, others may modernize or transpose the scene to a different period and use a dance to make this evident. There are even examples where historical dance is used for comic effect, when an anachronistic style is purposely chosen. This book focuses primarily on the training of an actor in a studio environment, considering the essential elements and sequences of steps, so that you can confidently work with these and the primary material of music, imagery, dance descriptions and costume. The research references are of a similarly primary nature, relating to the people who performed these dances when they were current, and so I have avoided a list of period-drama films. Considering these would be part of the next step in your training, taking the understanding developed through this work into the process of performance creation, considering the particular aim of the production in which you are being asked to perform dance dramatically. For this reason, I encourage you to learn the material alternating between different approaches, so you can adapt the material to different dramatic situations, rather than starting with the end product of a final performance.

Take Off

The world I am asking you to consider is historical, and needs to be reimagined for today and considered in a practical way. This book is not a detailed history text, so I openly admit to having taken some liberties to enable bold distinctions to be made, so that each chapter presents a definite style. I encourage you to consider other opinions of historical events and challenge reasons for their existence, and make a practical decision on what feels appropriate for the character, the play and the particular production.

To begin a dance routine, you often hear dance teachers scream numbers to count in the dancers:

'Five ... Six ... Seven ... Eight ...'

For the actor, I prefer to count down, as if you are launching your body into a new world, into something that, once given energy, could follow any rhythm and take any form.

So, I now invite you to enter the dimension of dance and make it dramatic:

'Three … Two … One … Dance!'

1
ANCIENT IDEAS:
DIONYSIAN ORCHESTRATION

Wandering stars revolve in chains:
Some orbit large and some are constrained.
Those with the lesser revolve with much speed,
While those with the larger will take more heed.

DIONYSIAN CHANT, INTERPRETED FROM THE
WORDS OF SOCRATES IN *THE TIMAEUS* BY PLATO

Within the Time Frame

- The classical period of Greece and Rome.

- From Homer to the Decline of the Roman Empire (approximately 800 BC to AD 500).

- Communities established around city states.

- Philosophical concepts made physical.

- Relating the individual to the cosmos.

- Dance related fundamentally to religious activities but also viewed by an audience in purpose-built amphitheatres.

- Groups working together rather than as solo performers.

An Actor Prepares to ...

- Work with the body as a three-dimensional whole.

- Move freely with no costume constraint.

- Connect to the concepts of time and space.

- Relate to other moving bodies in an energized abstract moving system.

- Work with physical impulses and shared responses.

- Consider a range of elemental movement qualities and making categories based on the movement styles.
- Perform to abstract musical structures.
- Establish prime directions in space.
- Consider the body as a spherical unit, revolving within a constantly moving world.
- Work as a combined moving group: the chorus.
- Use different shapes of the body to relate to space and time.
- Track the movement of the body in space.
- Create a character from abstract ideas: a divine being.
- Consider character as a choice, linking to a defined mask or mythical archetype.
- Combine with others in a dance dialogue.

Mystic Ritual

It is possible to visit the ruins of ancient theatres to return literally to the place where dance was once performed in a dramatic context, but the actual authentic dance still remains mystical and elusive. Philosophers of these times proposed theories relating to time, space and motion, so actors can use their imaginations to translate these into real physical sensations to make dance. In ancient theatre, dance was performed in the *orchesis*, translated as the English word *orchestra*. For the actor, this circular performing area combines two sensations: gathering in the physical world to their own breathing bodies, while reaching out into the open and beyond into the spiritual cosmos. In this circular space, actors were organized as a chorus: combining vocal arts with the physical art of moving in a stylized expressive way, connected to the drama. The ritual was presided over by the Priest of Dionysos, and he would appoint a figure with the name of 'Choregos' as the person in charge of this group to channel artistic ideas through performance. The medium for performance would equate to the activity we now call dance.

Dress for Dionysian Dramatic Dance

The clothing worn by the actors of ancient times very much resembled the style of the audience, with adaptations as required for the role being performed. The 'chiton' was basically a sheet of cloth, wrapped around, gathered and tied or attached with pins. Visual representations present many variations in how the cloth was cut, arranged, attached and belted, although the body could move freely.

Masks

Masks were part of the mystique of the ritual, either to hide individual identity, produce a group identity, or to take on the character of another being. The act of putting on a mask connected to the transformative power of theatre, both for the actors involved and the spectators gathered for the occasion.

The following Expressive Dance exercises do not require masks or historical costume, although this chapter requires a suspension of disbelief, so that abstract ideas can be made physical, and this requires an imaginative commitment to the ritualistic activity of performance.

Dancing with the Stars

Philosophers such as Plato proposed that the physical body needed to actively create energy to engage with the world.

Imagine the body producing its own energy, and that you can control how much of this is sent forth into the world. Even when standing still or in a static pose, how can you make your body emanate? Imagine that any walls have been removed, and you can sense further into an endless space beyond. Now feel the space above and around. Sense this first as a new sensation and then begin to explore with your physical limbs, as if you own everything in which you are exploring. How expansive can you be? How far can your limbs stretch to imaginatively extend beyond the physical reality and into the space of the cosmos: reaching for the stars, quite literally.

Laban Dance:

An internal need to move expands into outer space, alternating between gathering and scattering movements.

Circling Constellations

The ancient Greeks proposed the image of a frame surrounding the universe: a ring of fixed constellations. The 12 zodiac signs were believed to move as one balanced structure.

Explore this image of the zodiac constellations by imagining your own body with stars placed on each limb, at each joint – not only on the front of the body, but also the sides, the back, the top of the head and the soles of the feet. We can call these 'star-points'. Imagine you can vary their intensity, make a sequence of imagined energy emissions from one point to another, or use them as 'eyes' to sense the space and interact with others in the studio space. Use these exercises to explore the independent movement of the limbs making arcs in space. Consider how the whole body can operate as one orchestrated system. The aim is to develop control of your movement by increasing your awareness of precise locations on your own body surface.

Laban Dance:

Limbs of the body move in circular arcs, and the body is imagined contained within a kinesphere – a moving circle.

Orchestration

From random improvised movements of the body, see what physical connections can be made between different points, and how these points on the body may operate as a moving organism, balancing the shapes you are making with imaginary lines joining these dots. Play with different ways these 'star-points' can relate and respond to each other: maybe one foot connects to your shoulder blade; your elbow to your knee-cap; your nose to your chest, and so on.

- Now think about the central area around which all these stars are fixed: this is your world, your *personal space*.

- Now try moving this collection of stars around the room with you: you are contained within your own *physical boundary*.

- As you meet others in the studio, find ways to relate to each other, using the 'star-points' as your way to interact, but maintaining your own structure: you are making *social interaction*.

Laban Dance:

Your kinesphere may be contained or extended, remaining personal or becoming social.

The Ancient Planets as Seven Modes of Being: 'Wandering Stars'

Representing stars as dancing bodies connects to the ancient historical view of the cosmos as an ordered dance. The word 'planet' takes its meaning from the Ancient Greek for 'wandering stars'. Not thinking of them simply as glowing lights in the sky, the seven identified planets were given their own identities related to a specific way of moving as spherical objects, and shared their names and personalities with ancient mythical gods. The aim in this chapter is to create a human dance of the planets by exploring these planetary qualities physically, considering how the use of time and space can determine character in dance.

The movement of each planet has its own particular qualities, expressed by its spherical motion. This may be determined by the size of the moving sphere, whether it is expanding or contracting, and the speed of the revolving as limbs move within this sphere.

Questions to Consider when Making the Dance Dramatic

Making Revolutions

How can spherical motion represent a particular character?
How can a form of rotation have a personality?

Imagine your planet has its own power that makes it revolve. Imagine the 'star-points' are combining as one force, as one glowing globe. How can your body be made to feel like an orb? Revolve in every way possible. Sometimes allow your moves to expand and feel powerful as all limbs reach for the extremity of this shape. Sometimes let the energy be contained in a small area around your body, so that your planetary shape is defined as a smaller moving shape.

Now as you interact with those other 'wanderers', allow your response to each person to alter, so that you notice the size of the moving energy you come into contact with. Is this a large planet that you need to allow wide space to move around, or is this a small planet that can move within small spaces?

Let *Space* relate to the sensation of *Time.* Let the speed of your revolving match the size of your spatial being, so that expansive shapes move slower than smaller contained ones.

Laban Dance:

Contraction and expansion of the kinesphere.

Wandering Around

To physically realize the ancient definition of planets as eternal wandering stars, we need to consider the idea of proscribed tracks in the cosmos, which have settled into a repeatable pattern, and with each particular planet having its own course of movement. Those who believed the world to be fixed in one place would see the sun move each day from East to West, believing the orb to travel under the world, before returning in the East the next morning. So, too, the other planets would be seen to revolve around the fixed Earth.

For actors to take on the movement of globe-like planets, each individual must rotate around an imagined central axis, and simultaneously move as a rotating body. The orbiting may be all around one determined central place, as in a unified cosmos, or around other planets, such as orbiting moons. Both forms of orbiting will be valid for our dance training, as dances will have focal points in the performing space and around other dancing partners sharing the space.

Laban Dance:

Focal points in dance.

Cosmic Motion

In the system proposed by the ancient astronomer Ptolemy, the planets orbit in a clockwise direction. This circular clockwise motion can be established in the studio. So, as you revolve independently, rotating around your own imagined axis, explore different limbs taking the lead to move your whole moving-sphere on this clockwise track. As you stand facing into the centre of the room, it is your left side of the body that will lead into the space. Then begin to progress around the room, keeping the same pattern of revolving as you follow a track. The central area is kept clear, for this is the space around which all moving bodies in the room must orbit.

Laban Dance:

Central axis in space.

Space and Time Combined

Our aim is to find a way of moving around the room in a constant way, always in motion. The motion may slow down or speed up, but eventually the moving bodies should establish a rhythm that completes the action of the rotation in a regular pattern: moving through a sequence of moves that return to the beginning after a similar amount of time, but moved further along on the track.

Music of the Spheres

To support this exercise it may be helpful to introduce sound and music. It is sometimes easier to keep moving if there is some outside force giving an ongoing rhythm. Connecting to such a rhythm will not let us stop our motion once we set off. Music with a repetitive structure provides the constant flow so that the motion never stops. This could be percussive music, or mood music with repetitive strains, that allows each student to find their own rhythm within this structure.

Human Spheres

For all these exercises, try to imagine yourself as one whole moving body. All your limbs are in one sphere, encased within a ball, and you are thinking of how this shape is moving as a whole. This approach is different from learning dance as simply steps, or moving limbs in sequence. In my experience, this is often a concern that halts the exploratory way of engaging with dance. Once actors are required to adhere to an exact order of steps, a fear comes into the mind of the actor that makes them think they may make a wrong step. By starting with spherical motion, there is no wrong 'step' that can be made, as long as whatever movement is made is keeping the whole body moving. This is a different challenge: to ensure every part of the body remains part of the constant flow.

Using a Sphere-Prop

One way to keep this sphere shape constantly in mind is to use a prop that reminds you of what you are trying to achieve with your body movement. Everyday objects that are created in the shape of spheres can be used to assist actors to connect with this whole-body motion, for example a collection of sports balls of different sizes could be used in the studio.

The motion of the whole body should be used to move the ball around the room. Obviously the easiest way to hold the ball is in your hands, although you may find other ways to keep the prop and your body moving together. The most important thing is to explore how the rotating of the object can make your whole body move, as if you were inside the prop itself. Even with the ball in your hands, consider the arcs made by the arms; convey its motion with the bending of the knees and lunges of the legs; use the curving of the spine, the twisting of the hips, the leading of the head with the release of the neck, the arching of the shoulders, and the contracting of the chest, so that you fully connect to the motion of this prop being moved around the room. When using the prop, you are likely to become self-absorbed in your own world, and will ignore what is happening around you. So be reminded to reconnect with the social world, to sense how the motion you've created connects to those around you. Think about size, speed, travelling distance and the circular pattern propelling the body around the room.

Exchanging Props

Once you are projecting the spherical movement, while also interacting with others in the studio, you can experiment with exchanging your spherical motion by taking on somebody else's object, and giving them yours, to discover a different level of circular motion. Different sizes of object should influence the size of the gestures and movements made by the body: using a small object translates into small, tighter motions with many separate limbs moving at a quicker pace, while a very large object makes you move the larger limbs of your body, producing large, slower, more expansive unified motions. There will be many interpretations and motions between these two extremes. Movements of the limbs may alternate from being made near the centre of the sphere (*Laban Dance: Central Motion*) or to the edge of this sphere (*Peripheral Motion*) or cutting between the edge and the centre (*Transversal Motion*).

Size System

A spatial system can be created based on the relationship between these faster and slower moving bodies moving around a central area. Larger spheres travel more distance in one rotation but at a slower speed, while smaller spheres move through less space in one revolution but at a quicker pace. Each sphere can be allocated a specific track around the room, with smaller, quicker and more confined movements gravitating closest to a central area, whizzing around in small inner tracks, and those with slower, large gesticulations, necessitating more space and room to flow, will be further out, away from the central area, following an outer track. Let the awareness of the size of spheres govern which track each moving body claims as its own, in this shared circular-clockwise-moving system. Establish relationships to each other in this size-ordered space.

The moving bodies should try to create balance now – evenly distanced from each other, both as circular tracks moving away from the centre in gradients from fast to slow, and between bodies sharing the same tracks, such as those sharing the fast inner-track movers, or the slower outer-tracks, or medium track movers spread accordingly between the outer and the inner tracks. You may measure in time how long it may take for each body to complete a full revolution around the central area – and consider the mathematical relationship between the different moving objects: for example, it may be found that a smaller sphere may complete six revolutions in the time it takes the outer larger sphere to complete its first revolution back to place. To help create this, you may stop and start the flow – by stopping and starting the music, for example. Count how many revolutions each body makes while the music is being played for a certain amount of time. Compare the number of revolutions made by other moving bodies in this same amount of time. Consider how this appears physically in space – how many revolutions are needed to return to the same place. This awareness is starting to make connections and relationships in a dynamic system.

Graphing the Track

Once this moving system feels ordered and organized in space and time, the actors should now place their ball-props down on the floor where they feel is appropriate, in relation to the movement of all those around them. There should still be a circular area left empty in the centre of the room, where a spare ball could now be placed to represent the Earth around which the other planets are imagined to orbit. The placing of the ball-props on the floor is to create a two-dimensional map of these concentric spheres travelling around the room. Spread out the ball-props evenly, while maintaining their relationships, so that they can be markers of the track. These different movement qualities come into operation when a moving body enters that particular track.

Floor Tracks

So now the type of movement will be decided by being in a particular place in space. The body will be styled by the spherical motion of each particular track when the body is moving in that place in the room. Begin by remaining in the track where you were operating as your own spherical object. Don't forget the sensation of moving as an abstract object, although the human social connection is now important, as you have a personality, and while moving in a similar way, engage with others you pass who are moving in other tracks. The flow of motion can now be in both directions: both the usual clockwise and in reverse. It is worth thinking that the dominant forward motion remains as clockwise, because this is the way you want to be moving in essence around the room, but you have a choice to reverse and relate to others around you throughout your journey. Now you can venture into the other tracks, and take on the spherical rotation of those particular tracks. If you start on the outer edge, you will rotate faster as you move towards the centre, and moving from the centre to the edge, your revolving will become less intense and more expansive.

Share these sensations with the others you meet on each track. Any meetings or collisions can develop into moments where you unify together, almost as joined as a new revolving sphere. You may find you move into another track as you become aware of other movers around you – some coming at you faster, others slowing you down and pulling you into their track. The central area is like a 'black hole' that you should avoid, but you will spin very close, and this energy of spiralling towards the fast centre should also propel you back into the slower tracks extending to the outer edges. It is important to visualize the circular tracks, orbiting the central area, getting progressively larger towards the perimeter of the room. These tracks equate approximately to the Ptolemaic design of the universe, which has the planets moving on a fixed track around the centre.

What the group have represented physically in the studio can be likened to how the Ancient Greeks organized their idea of the cosmos into a system of movement, which astronomers such as Ptolemy would graph as a geocentric model. This was not only considered as a scientific model for understanding planetary motion, to measure the time taken for the revolutions of planets believed to be orbiting around the Earth, but also an explanation for the type of forces given to each planet. The planets are dancing around the Earth, and their motion is producing music, not heard by mankind as such, given the name *Musica Universalis* or 'The Music of the Spheres'. This ancient astrology connected to the idea of different qualities specifically identified in the named Olympian gods, and these gods had very human characteristics, as found in the myths and references in ancient drama.

Becoming Gods

This revolving object can be imagined as a god with a human-like personality expressed through the movement and physical power that can affect anyone who may come into their sphere. This physical power can extend beyond the planet's own physical body to be an 'aura' surrounding the moving object. As a god, they have an area which they govern, which we can call the god's *domain*, and a way of expressing themselves always in one form of expression, which we can call the god's *character*. Each planet-god will use a different mode of movement, and then each mode can have an associated style of dance.

Secret Seven

The seven planets were imagined to be part of a movement system that related to the way they rotated, and the speed at which they progressed and orbited around the world. The Moon, which we still believe to be revolving around the Earth, was considered to be the first planet that would be met on the journey from the Earth into the cosmos. Following the Moon's sphere, there would be Mercury, Venus, the Sun, Mars, Jupiter and Saturn. Each planet's motion was attributed to a concentric sphere rotating clockwise around the Earth, which was fixed in the centre of this universe. Following our simplistic physical

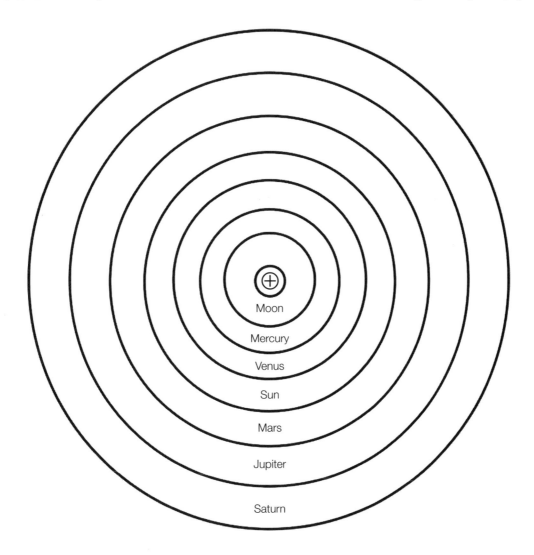

realization of this system in the studio, each planet can now be made into a dancing being with a connection between the ancient god and the planetary motion. After the Moon, we will consider Mercury to be the smallest and quickest planet, and Saturn to operate as the largest and most expansive planet, taking more time to rotate and complete a revolution. The other planets will fit in order between these two extremes and be given their equivalently sized spherical motion.

Sphere Characteristics

Below is a table of some pointers to guide the movement of the planets in this spherical system. Keep reminding each other that the movement must be like a dance, and connect always to the types of moves that were created from the abstract exploratory exercises.

If you are **Saturn,** the largest sphere, how would you be as a person dancing in this orb? Your limbs would all be connected into one large moving shape. How would the slowness make the spherical motion? Making large arcs as you travel around your axis, with limbs sagging and being lifted with care as you heave yourself around as a gigantic globe requiring all your controlled energy to move yourself around laboriously; rocking and creaking as you let the heaviness take you into your ancient mode of movement; meeting each other as everything else moves too fast around you, and taking an age to actually travel around the room; realizing every turn of every body part in your body shape which seems to take forever to make a full revolution.

In contrast, **Mercury**, the fastest-moving planet, has erratic retrograde motion, going in different directions around the fast track, appearing to visit other planets very briefly, then off in another direction like quicksilver, as different body parts lead your motion to make other tiny speedy completed rotations, so fast that the mover is not aware of the slower-moving objects, and has the alertness to dodge them and move around them, avoiding collision at the very last moment.

How can the fighting quality of the planet **Mars** still be placed into movements within a sphere?

How can the saucy moves attached to the goddess **Venus** be contained in a rotating globe?

As the brightest star, the **Sun** may be able to extend its beams through the entire cosmos, and the philosopher Aristotle was one of those who considered the Sun to be the central planet in the cosmos. But, to maintain this Ptolemaic system we have created in the studio, the Sun's physical orb itself is to be considered in the medium size, and the movement made must connect to a medium-sized glowing body, from which benevolent blessings can be extended to those all around.

Jupiter is a ruling god in this system, and to create a spherical dance display by this majestic king, the body in motion must find power in the large slow revolving motion made between the age-old Saturn and fiery Mars.

The Sun is placed between Mars and Venus, and in some way can be considered as a buffer between these two gods that have passionate feelings for each other.

The important thing at this stage is that each actor creates their own system, with movement quality differences for themselves. If you have worked in small groups to establish your own sphere dance for your planetary god, it is a good idea to then perform this to the others, and for everyone to have a go at physically taking on board your choices, then allowing the dance of this particular planet to take over the entire studio. I would suggest that the group follow the order from the largest to the smallest, as beginning with the slow, enlarged movements may bring everyone together as one unified whole. Keep being reminded to be spherical and to remember a basic characteristic from the table, or other words that come to mind.

You may find a relevant piece of music for each planet. An obvious example from classical music would be *The Suite of the Planets* by Gustav Holst, where each planet has a particular theme, but it is interesting for actors to select music they are familiar with that connects to the motion they have created.

1.1: Planet Movement Analysis

Groups		How do you express these characteristics within a unified spherical movement?
Roman	*Greek*	*Character*
Saturn	Cronus	Melancholy and dignity, the oldest god
Jupiter	Zeus / Jove	Majesty and power, the ruling god
Mars	Ares	Fighting with anger, the god of war
Sol (Sun)	Apollo	Generosity and kindness, the god of beaming light
Venus	Aphrodite	Seductive and salacious, the goddess of love
Mercury	Hermes	Speedy and excitable, the messenger god
Luna (Moon)	Selene	Waxing and waning, the goddess of reflecting light

Moon Dancing

Because the Moon was believed to be moving through different transformative phases, you may find you can create different versions of dance within this one 'lunar' mode. Beginning with a new Moon, imagine how pure and ethereal you can make your movements. The Moon when it is full is seen to be the most powerful. As the Moon waxes and wanes, power changes, and characters may be controlled by this power, from the chaste nymphs of the goddess Diana to the wild witches and werewolves of Hecate. The word 'lunatic' implied that insanity was connected to the Moon's influence; so, too, can other personalities be imagined as being controlled by the other planetary powers. Even elements that make up the physical world on the Earth can have particular modes of movement.

Four Elements

Plato believed that all physical material in the world was constructed from the Four Elements. Within the Sphere System, the Four Elements are given different geometric shapes which we now call the Platonic Solids. Laban would also consider ways to move in particular organized systems, which can be imagined as 'scaffoldings' developing sequences called 'scales'. Exercises can be developed that explore these particular geometric shapes, attaching different qualities to architectural shapes and linking to human personality traits.

1.2: The Four Elements

Elements	Shape	Quality
Fire	Tetrahedron (pyramid) (4 sides) – 4 corner-points	Erratic
Air	Octahedron (diamond) (8 sides) – 6 corner-points	Suspended
Earth	Cube (box) (6 sides) – 8 corner-points	Solid
Water	Icosahedron (20 sides) –12 corner-points	Fluid

First Steps

We know that in the ancient world, dance was included in many social activities. For example, the *pyrrhic mode* before fighting or to celebrate a battle, the *lyrical modes* connected to love and marriage, and the frenzied *bacchic modes* used to create a feeling of ecstasy during religious rituals. Depictions of figures in flowing robes in murals or on vases are often interpreted as representing dancers performing at these events. Although these provide a sense of the movement and shapes created with the body, they cannot be used to reconstruct specific step patterns. The rhythm of the steps needs to connect to the modes of movement appropriate for that event, and each step will transfer the body into a particular direction.

Seven Motions

Plato, in *The Timaeus*, proposes that there are seven principal directions governing all motion.

These seven motions can work as a basic list of directional movements to categorize all forms of dance steps.

He lists the following directions:

Forward – 1
Backward – 2
Side to Side – 3 and 4
Up and Down – 5 and 6
Turn Around – 7

It is worth exploring movement in these seven ways, as every dance can be made up of a combination of these units of direction. It is important to first let the body explore and understand these motions independently of each other. You must make a clear choice as to which direction you are moving your body in. Take as much time as possible to move in one of these directions. For example, move forwards in space until you meet an obstacle, then choose an alternative direction.

When asked to move around the room, students will normally first choose to walk forward; this therefore should be considered our first direction. Backwards is automatically chosen as the second, being a direct opposite. Through doing this exercise, you will find a balance between forwards and backwards, one side with the other, and upwards and downwards motion. (*Laban Dance: Dimensional Scale*).

Having systematically gone through these prime motions, you may now wish to go in a diagonal direction. This is simply a combination: sideward motion with either forward or backward.

The following exercises will only use the prime directions to create dance patterns for solos, duets and groups.

Chorus Group Movement

We mentioned that the group of performers in the Ancient Greek *orchesis* were named the chorus. The word chorus connects to the circular space where they performed, and the idea of dancing with circles is important for this technique of including everyone in the activity, both the others in the group and the spectators, seated around the circle.

Different directions can be used by the chorus group to create different formations.

Unified Chorus

Begin by everybody moving together in the same direction, with a chorus leader dictating which way. The leader, the *choregus*, chooses from the seven principal directions. As a member of the chorus, you need to be ready to change direction and sense which of the seven ways the leader will take you. The aim is to be as unified as possible. After a while, the leader can relinquish this power and signal to another member of the group to take over.

Repeat this exercise until as many people who wish to be leader have had a go. Once you have established working as a unified chorus, one actor will be identified to work separate to this chorus.

Introducing Thespis: One Actor Interacting with the Chorus

It is believed that the first actor, Thespis, worked as a solo performer interacting with a unified chorus. This idea can create a new dynamic between the different directions, with the chorus continuing with this unified movement working in opposition with one solo actor.

While the chorus works together under the direction of their *choregus*, Thespis moves independently within the group. Always trying to move in an opposing direction to that of the chorus, the solo performer must also keep choosing to alternate between the seven directions. This exercise can become a game, where if the solo performer moves in the same direction as the chorus, the role of Thespis must be handed to a new player.

Repetitive Sequence as a Solo Performer

Once understood, these seven directions can now be organized in a set pattern, forming a spatial structure that will be the essence of your own solo dance sequence. This can train the actor to remember dance as a series of directions taken by the whole body, rather than simply steps of the feet. Each individual will have their own combinations of the seven Platonic motions in any order, but they must keep performing this same sequence around the studio. How much time is spent on each direction does not matter, but when your track meets that of another dancer and you are required to change direction, it must maintain the sequence of directions you had previously decided.

Dialogue Dance Structure

Dialogue is a conversational exchange between two or more people. The basic idea of a dialogue in Ancient Greek philosophy has been attributed to the philosopher Socrates, the teacher of Plato. Through discussion and debate with his pupils, a dialogue structure would develop where an answer to one question would lead to the next. This dialogue approach can be applied to movement interaction on stage between actors, who must develop a skill of physically reacting naturally to the action of other characters and situations.

The next exercise will use our seven Platonic motions in a Socratic-style dialogue form. Small groups of solo performers should interact with each other in an 'answer and response' format, allowing the movement choices they make to progress the action.

The simplest form of dialogue is between two people. One actor can make one move in one direction, the other responds.

Now that you are familiar with the seven Platonic directions, use these to have a dialogue with a partner. The sequence now is decided by how you wish to respond to the particular direction given by your partner. One person begins and makes one move, choosing one of the seven directions. The partner now must make another move. Alternate between each other constantly, but keep it simple, by only making one move at a time, always in a different direction each time. Build up a sequence until you have a series of moves linked together, ideally using all the seven options. Different directions will take you towards or away from your partner, will connect you more with the partner or put you into parallel patterns, while others will take you into opposing tracks, making you break away and extend the space.

Once you have created a sequence with your partner comprising a number of moves, return to the beginning and practise this movement dialogue, so that the change from one partner to another becomes seamless. Afterwards, discuss what certain directions felt like to you, as responses to what the other person did.

Dances will be constructed from these elements, and partner dances will always depend on this connection between different directions occurring simultaneously. Certain patterns when repeated will produce a spatial rhythm that we can consider as expressing a certain mode of movement, which the two dancers (or more) can maintain.

Greek Feet

It is assumed that the Greek chorus would vocalize as they performed. The poetry could be divided into stressed and unstressed syllables, which are called metric feet. Maybe the Greek chorus while reciting the poetry would move their feet to emphasize the rhythms of the verse?

One option would be to make short steps into space on unstressed syllables of words (**da**), and make long steps when on the accented stress of the word (**DUM**).

For example:

To**day**, we **dance** in **An**cient **Greece**
To-DAY, we DANCE in AN-cient GREECE
Da DUM da DUM da DUM da DUM

This far-fetched literal interpretation of 'metric feet' is a useful exercise for actors to explore stressed and non-stressed accents while stepping. This will be a skill needed in dance forms that use the feet to match rhythms in the music, and to create repetitive rhythms.

Using combinations of accents on syllables, step the following rhythms. While walking, emphasize the stressed accents into the floor and make the unstressed steps as light as you can.

da	unstressed
DUM	stressed
da-DUM	iambic (speech)
da-da	pyrrhic (war)
DUM-da	trochaic / choraic (dance)
DUM-DUM	spondaic (libation)
da-DUM-DUM	bacchic (ecstasy)
DUM-da-da	dactyl (named as the finger joints: long, short, short)

Ancient Dance Composition

With this technical knowledge and the imaginative responses from the Expressive Dance exercises, combine the three ideas of the Moving Sphere character, the Element Quality and the Direction Dialogue, working in small groups to compose a style of dance appropriate for a ritualistic moment in theatre performance.

Create a Show Dance that combines metric rhythm, geometric shapes and flowing circles, to communicate ideas connected to the character of an ancient god and their respective elemental forces.

The Fighting Mode: Warlike Weapons

This mode relates to the idea of *pyrrhic*.

The metrical feet used will be two short syllables, as two short stabs: **da-da**.

Speak the word 'py-rrhic' under your breath to keep this rhythm going, which may speed up or slow down, or come in short starts and bursts.

- Choose a planetary sphere to govern the domain and give you a character.

- Example: Mars is an obvious planet for this mode, although all planets can find a version for their attacking moves.

- Select which elements you will express with your Movement Flow: Fire and Earth relate to the typical depiction of Mars.
- Create a sequence for a Direction-Dialogue. Convey the idea of attack and defence, using opposing forces.
- Combined mode: Mars, Earth and Fire, Forward and Backward.

The Lyrical Mode: Elegies and Love Poems

Lyrics are poetically flowing in balance and harmony and may be used to communicate ideas about love.

A combination of the trochee (from the word for 'wheel') or choree (from the word choreus, for '*dance*') (**DUM-da**) may also roll into the dactylic metre (**DUM-da-da**).

   Example: the Planet Venus, with the elements of Water and Air, and a dialogue with directions that work in harmony, with balance from side to side, and lilting up and down.

The Ecstatic Mode: Bacchic Libations

Dance may be used in ancient ritual to change from one state to another, to move to an extreme level of focused energy, when the performers reach a heightened state in spiritual worship, making offerings to divine beings, such as the chorus of women in Euripides' *The Bacchae*.

- Use the different stepping rhythms of the serious spondee (**DUM-DUM**) and a triple (**da-DUM-DUM**) as a choric chant, which could occur between the other more ordered modes of pyrrhic and lyric.
- Element shapes can be changed wildly as a chaotic dance is produced, demonstrating abandon to the whirling motion with the seventh motion of turning in place.

Summary of Laban Dance Ideas

Kinesphere

- Moving in a sphere shape.

The idea of the body being contained within a globe-like structure can be used to analyse the whole body moving in space.

Extension and Contraction

- Large sphere or small sphere.

Rotation

- Around a line in space.
- Around body parts.
- Forward focus.

Directions and Dimensions

- Seven directions.
- Four dimensions.

Movement Qualities

- Relating to shape.

Step Rhythms

- Stressed and unstressed.

Historical Evidence: Satyr Plays

The Pronomos Vase has been considered as one of the most important surviving pieces of pictorial evidence for ancient theatre. Dated from the fifth century BC, it depicts what is believed to be a satyr play, one of the plays that would accompany the tragedies at the drama festivals. These satyr plays relied heavily on physical performance and dance as part of the narrative, and the chorus of satyrs moved as one group of actors with masks, reacting to the events in the story. They had a shared movement style, mixing with the beastly element of being a half-animal creature. Their dance was given the name of 'sikinni', connecting to the steps of the goat, with skipping and jumping.

This type of satyr chorus appears in Sophocles, *The Trackers*. The god Apollo tricks the chorus of satyrs to follow a scent to the cave where Hermes has been born. The comic dance style is based on searching using smell, and becomes vulgar as the energy of the dance increases the foul odour of the satyrs themselves! Apollo controls the movement from above, with the satyrs being led by their noses into making collisions created by changes of direction.

Summary: Ritual Energy and Modes of Movement

This previous historical example of dance in satyr drama has taken us very far from the idea of a divine harmonic cosmic motion with which we began this chapter. With only fragmentary evidence for dance forms, we have explored general modes rather than specific dance reconstructions. However, by exploring these concepts in an imaginative way, the actor has considered the movement of the body as a whole, using space and time to alter movement qualities and established a dynamic system for working as a solo performer and in a group, without really learning any dance steps as such. All these elements will be used as a basis for dances in other periods, when we have more historical evidence to construct specific steps.

Further Research Springboard

- Text:
  - *The Timaeus* by Plato explains the ancient philosophy of motion, considering how certain things have a natural movement in directions and modes.
- Image:
  - Plato's spherical cosmology is visually represented by Ptolemy. Consider images that graph these movement patterns and the crystal shapes associated with the elements.
  - The Promonos Vase depicts actors with masks and theatrical gestures, linking gods to human personalities.
- Music:
  - Select music with changes of pulses and rhythms, sequential repetitions, and different modes.
  - Ancient modal ideas have inspired present-day composers such as Michael Nyman, Philip Glass and Ludovico Einaudi.
  - Works such as *The Planets* by Gustav Holst explore musical themes for cosmic characteristics.

2
MEDIEVAL REALMS: FEUDAL FORMATIONS

We are amazed; and thus long have we stood
To watch the fearful bending of thy knee,
Because we thought ourself thy lawful king:
And if we be, how dare thy joints forget
To pay their awful duty to our presence?

KING RICHARD SPEAKS TO HENRY BOLINGBROKE,
SHAKESPEARE'S *THE TRAGEDY OF KING RICHARD II*,
ACT 3, SCENE 3

Within the Time Frame

- Middle Ages in Europe from the collapse of the Roman Empire through to the fifteenth century.
- Feudal systems of hierarchy of power: designated rulers and followers.
- Defence structures in physical buildings: walled cities, castles and fortresses.
- Secular celebrations for civic occasions with cultural codes to emphasize hierarchy.

An Actor Prepares to …

- Consider leadership: physically leading the group.
- Consider how to be a follower in dance terms: a dance chain.
- Sense a shared flow in the dance: leaving and returning to this imagined energy.
- Take instruction from a dancing leader and sense active communication in motion.
- Learn strategies for creating structures made by the body in motion, and tactics for varying movement choices while in action.
- Defend, protect, contain and control through use of the moving body in space, using circular formations.

- Learn dance steps as bricks to build larger structures.

- Begin using handhold to communicate intention to partners.

- Analyse improvised dance steps as changes of body weight.

- Learn how to respect partners in dance.

- Establish gestural codes for a defined social group.

- Understand how social hierarchy can relate to spatial organization.

Defining the Social Area

It may be helpful to begin this chapter with the image of the ruined castle, once a necessary stronghold and powerful defence. We cannot physically take the fallen stones and build the fortresses that held these people in a particular formation, but we can imagine how human bodies may have connected with other bodies, and how these connections would give an appearance of a structured world.

A medieval realm had prescribed physical boundaries that were also upheld by movement patterns made by those belonging to that society.

The notion of leadership will be explored in the dance of this section, both being constantly challenged and changing. Dance will be considered as a display of social harmony. The presentation of tensions within these structures is one way that makes the dance dramatic, and dance forms in this chapter have been selected to visually present the political and social elements of medieval feudal hierarchy.

Expressing Feudal Order

Feudal order has the principal idea of a leader at the top of a ladder of importance. Others in the realm all have a place in this hierarchy, each with a duty and a function in the social world, but unifying as an ordered group in a political way to defend themselves against attacks from other locations, be they different clans, other nations, or even opposing factions from within.

Ring Fencing

The circle is now being considered as a defensive shape. By linking to the people on either side of you holding hands, you no longer feel a free-moving sphere, but have a place in a communal structure. As a group, you are in effect making a wall, a barricade, with an inside and outside. You become aware of the space inside that you are protecting with your bodies.

Circle Capture

Stand holding hands with everyone in the studio. See the space that you now have captured. You can look across and see others who are in the same society. They are working as a group defining and marking out this space, feeling safe. The Great Hall of medieval castles would have had a central fire, around which such circular formations may have been made, but the actor must imagine making such spaces without such a setting. Consequently, the first exercises in this chapter will train the group to form and re-form the circle shape in many locations, and at different times. This circular shape should be stored in the physical memory of the actor, as it may need to be sensed hidden behind certain movement patterns, even when not always being physically created by the dancing bodies.

The Call to Arms

Begin by moving independently around the room, randomly changing directions and focus. At a given moment you will be summoned to form a circle. When the fanfare calls, or when the drum beats, immediately move and stand in the communal circle. Form the circle as quickly as you can as a group, but always moving with an awareness of the others in the room, and sensing how the shape comes into being.

This is a good device for ensemble playing – knowing that a structure exists in your mind that can be quickly formed physically in the space so that every person is included. A circle can always open wider to include as many as possible in the room. It should not matter at this stage in which order the people stand; in fact this exercise requires you to be aware of everyone together as one group and not be so aware of who the particular people are joining to either side of you. The shape of the circle formed should be as geometrically perfect as possible.

Shatter Stability

Once this point of stability has been reached, another signal from the instructor should shatter this shape. Chaos should return immediately, so that the order created by the shape disappears into the past.

Repeat this exercise of forming and disbanding the circle, with the instructor altering the length of time between signals so that everyone has moved to different places in the room each time.

New Order

Recapturing something that is lost is sometimes futile, and human bodies in a studio cannot simply rewind movement as if recorded and replayed. So always try to create a new form of the circle rather than restore the former order. In this way, each creation of a circle should always feel like a new formation each time, although you may find that patterns may start to form, as people will start to respond in a particular way suited to their preferred habitual movements.

Energized Geometry: 'Active Surrounding'

Repetition of these types of circle exercises should train the group to be able to form geometrically perfect circles when required. The moment when you all stand side by side, we can call a moment of 'active surrounding'. To make it 'interactive' you need to take hands with the others in the group, and keep a feeling of motion even in a static shape.

Hands Fast or Slow

You can try two systems for taking hands with the others on the circumference of the circle: either joining hands gradually as you feel you have formed the circle, or taking your place standing in the circle and, when everyone is in place, only then all joining hands together. This second approach allows you to place yourself into the circle anywhere around the circumference, and can therefore enable some last-minute decisions, allowing you to see a vacant space and slot into the group. It can give the fun feeling of a game, and some players enjoy teasing the others by leaving unknown until the last moment which gap they will fill. This is a worthwhile approach to keep the group alert, and the test of success is how precise the linking occurs at the last moment: full marks if this is exactly together as a unified agreed moment in time and space, when the bodies are all in place. This exact action approach trains the idea of collaborative closure – rather like placing the full stop at the end of a sentence, being in exact rhythm as a chorus, or closing the final consonant of a word in a song altogether at the end of the phrase. This takes us into the disciplined metric ordering of time and space, one necessary technique needed for the execution of certain communal dances.

The other approach, where you meet hands gradually as you walk into your position, is the one which will be needed for dances which have an element of social negotiation: the circle is formed as you realize you have made a small connection with one person, which will make part of the whole, and the expansion into a group formation will grow organically. For this method, introduce a rule: once a hand joins with another person, this link cannot be broken. There is a temptation to open up the link to let someone else in who finds themselves straggling outside. If we imagine that it would not be socially acceptable to then cut into the space closed by the hands held between two people it gives another challenge to the activity, as all individuals must be brought into the circle, but once a connection has been made it should not be broken, so the hand joining should respect the others moving in the space and have an awareness of all those coming to form the group circle.

Flowing Motions of the Circle

Once you and your group have mastered the idea of forming a static circle at any given time, the next requirement is to keep in motion as you move into the circle, while walking within this circular pattern. Walking should be in a forward direction, and the circle should move towards the left side of the moving bodies, in a clockwise motion. At another signal from the instructor you can be released from this circle, continuing to walk, changing direction immediately if you wish, but holding onto the sensation of having moved in a circle with your bodies. Even making this chaotic movement you should imagine that you now have this shape in your body, and can bring it forth whenever required to link with others.

Although the idea of always performing a perfect circle may be a beautiful idea, it may be difficult to make this idea dramatic, so I want to introduce some exercises which create an active dynamic tension within the group, using interaction from actors wanting to play with the shape to develop techniques of leading and following in the dance.

Pushing the Boundary

Allow the group, while still holding hands, to move anywhere around the room, keeping linked but not caring for the shape that is being made. At a signal from the instructor the group should re-establish the perfectly shaped circle.

Moving Target

Someone may be placed into this sacred central space, and imagine that the circle of bodies is protecting them. One of you will become a moving central figure and the circle protects that person by surrounding them. The instructor may shout a name of someone in the group. It is now this player's realm that is being created. On hearing the name, everyone moves to form a circle around this body. This trains the awareness of the space and volume needed around a central axis.

Many Motions

You may then select more than one person to be circled, shouting two or more names. Or the instructor may introduce a secret way of identifying the central person with a small gesture, a tap on the back, even a look in the eyes – and then the chosen central person may just stop in motion, so that those others moving around must circle them and keep moving. Now the moving bodies have to decide which individual will be their central person. You can leave this up to chance as to whether one circle has more people than the others making the ring, or you can be challenged with the need to make them a balanced number.

Creative Circling

There are lots of other creative ways to develop interaction with such circles, and testing the ability of making the circle a protective ring. Come up with your own ideas to suit the personalities in the group, and indeed the space you have to play with. You may wish to create inner and outer rings; or introduce rules to govern the number of people allowed; you may wish to explore different ways of making the circle shape with different parts of the body. All such exercises contribute to a physical awareness of the communal shapes and structures which then can be considered as the skeleton of the body of the dance.

Always ...

- Always remember it is the moving bodies that are making the shape.
- Always make sure the moving body is actively keeping the shape alive.

Don't ...

- Don't let the shape be an unenergized neutral, but rather a moment of suspension of a circular shape in space.

Variations to Make it Dynamic:

- What happens if the central point changes location around the room?
- Can the outer circle rotate and maintain the shape around a moving central axis?

Social Circles

All these exercises have been based on the idea of 'self-protection'. Through these explorations of maintaining the circle with moving bodies, you have developed awareness of the shape as something which protects what the group has identified as being important. But what happens if there are forces that want to attack this area from the outside and invade this sacred space?

Who's Behind You?

So now, while standing in your circle, and holding hands with those making up this circle, consider the outside of this circle shape. Holding hands in the circle means that it is not really possible for you to turn around to see what is behind you. You are prevented from fully knowing what is going on behind you, and indeed those next to you on either side cannot give you that information either. Those opposite you, however, on the other side of the circle, have more chance of knowing what is behind your side of the circle. In fact, as a defensive shape, protection comes from the fact that while dancing facing into the circle you can see everyone in the group and respect the shape of the inside, but also you can see what is happening around the circle on the outside on the opposite side: within this communal system, you also have to rely on the others to protect your own back. So be aware of any invasion from outside.

Dance of Death

You may wish to make up some similar games to explore this notion of protecting from the outside. For example, by delineating an area in the room to be protected, with bodies moving chaotically, an 'invader' may be selected. Whenever the invader moves towards this area, the others make a barrier, striving for a circular barrier with hands joined.

The invader could imagine being the hand of death, setting out to touch the shoulder of one of the dancers midway through the dance; to give a medieval game context, you could, for example, imagine this figure to be a personification of the plague setting out to strike the person dead! All the circle dancers must continue their steps in the rotating circle, but if the invader gets close, those on the opposite side who can see this must give a shout. The shout prevents the invader making the hit. The invader must retreat, and prepare to make another invasion. Of course these are exactly like children's playground games. Introducing them into the rehearsal of a dance, however, makes this a much more complex task for an actor. You must continue dancing, keeping the perfect form of the shape and the order of the steps, while continuing with an awareness of all of the fellow actors and the space around the dance.

Now that we have trained in making a circle-shape expressive for the group as a whole, we shall introduce the notion of independent leadership – and for this we will consider the line formation.

Leading with Lines

The circle is the shape we have been exploring, but we are now going to imagine that this can continue even when our hands are no longer completely linked, and instead there is one person given the actual job of leading the line. A line of dancers will now be considered as an *open-ended circle*.

Left Leads

Start in your circle. Give motion to the circle. For traditional reasons we shall ask for the motion to move to the left, so that forward motion is clockwise around the circle.

It has been suggested that this moving to the left connects to the movement of the planets and the sun around the Earth, which relates to a standard world-view of the medieval period. From an actor's viewpoint, it is going to be helpful if you adopt a belief which makes a distinction between left and right, so that left moving is the first motion forward, and that moving to the right is connected to the retrograde, the movement backward in space. It could be noted that the heart is on the left side of our bodies, and you solely lead with your heart! It is indeed more useful to think of something connected to the body rather than the feet, as we are still concerned with dance being shapes made by the whole human body in motion, rather than steps on the floor.

Sway into Action

If your circle has come to a standstill, then begin motion by swaying the group from one side to the other. Motion in a circle requires that everyone is moving in the same sidewards direction, but the communication of that direction is given along the circumference and not across the circle. This will become vital for learning step sequences in a circle. *In a circle, avoid learning direction by what is in front of you, but rather from what is to your side.* Look around the circle and imagine the group moving as one unit. You can emphasize this sequence in games that pass signals along the circumference edge, making joined-up patterns in a relay formation where one person looks to the left, and passing this on all around the circle until it reaches the leader once more. To help make this initiation of the movement secure, in these classes I suggest that you decide to pass everything to the left. When music becomes a part of this swaying, then the left-side motion will accompany the first beat of the measure, and in this way the left side will become connected to the natural accent or stress.

Once the sway has become understood as an initiating move by one leader, the leader can then let his left hand drop from the circle. This person has a left hand as a free hand. On the next sway to the left, the leader continues walking. If you are the leader you will have your left hand free, so lead into the space to the left and let the others follow you, linked onto you by your right hand. This walk continues in the left-side direction, going anywhere around the room. The group is required to follow. Now the walks continue forward. Wherever you, as the leader, take this line of joined-up people is fine, but in the end, the line must join up again, and the leader will take the right hand of the person at the end of the circle-line.

No matter what deviating shapes have been made on this journey by the leader, once the circle is re-formed, the group should ensure this is as geometrically perfect as possible, and balanced evenly with the number in the group. Once the circle is formed from the left forward walking, the group should sway again, going back to the right then on again to the left, and continuing, with one pulse for each sway. Another person can now take up the leadership of this line, and on a subsequent left-sway that person can set off and take the circle-line on a different journey into other shapes before returning to the communal circle.

It is possible to have more than one leader. They can then journey as smaller lines, and then meet with the large circle at the end.

The leader needs to be very aware of the end of their line of people. As the larger circle is re-formed, it is important how the leader guides their line into the larger shape. As the leader, you should believe that your physical entity stretches completely to the end of the line of people in your independent group.

After a few excursions returning to the one large circle, split into these smaller groups with fewer numbers, and make smaller circles. A leader sets off and connects back into this smaller circle many times, changing leader within the small group each time, swaying in between so that the route is propelled by the idea of a circle. Reduce the number of people in the group, to a minimum of three people, so that the switch of leadership becomes almost immediate, maybe even allowing only one sway to the right before the next person takes over. *Make sure, above all, that the sense of the circle is never lost.* Even when you are leading a line of people, you should still be aware of how your motion to the left continues as if you were still moving in a circle.

The Follower is Formed

In a large circle, it is easy to see the pathway that you need to follow. It is less obvious with fewer people in the line. We will need to keep this in mind when we explore moving as much smaller units, as even a couple dancing together will be considered a small circular unit of one leader with only one follower.

Historical Dance

Chains of Being: From Top to Bottom

What is the historical significance of exploring these techniques of making circles, being aware of the circle formation, and leading into other places in the dancing arena to make shapes?

There are many pictorial examples of people joined in circles from the medieval period, and we assume this to be social dancing. The idea of a circle representing the community is relevant, but of more importance is that within this group there may be someone who is elected as being responsible for leading, and always having the good of the whole group in mind.

One such dance supporting this notion of social leadership is featured in the wall painting in the Palazzo in Siena. This fourteenth-century mural, entitled *The Effects of Good Government in a Secure City*, depicts a group of people with hands joined, making patterns, while someone is playing a tambourine with their mouth wide open – presumably singing along.

Dance can be related to the main theme of good government in this art. Some historians have suggested that the dancers in this central position in the painting represent the politicians of the city, maybe even actually dancing to show their skill as good governors. At the very least, it is possible to identify a symbolic link to the nine governors of Siena of that time. The mural includes depictions of other usual activities occurring in the city at the time, so we can assume that this type of dancing was performed in the streets. The artist has captured the dance at a moment where the arms of the leading couples are lifted, allowing for a passing under the arms. It is probable that at this moment a new person from the group could take on the leading of the whole line.

Follow my Leader

In this improvised line dance through the streets, how would a leader pass on this message to make this move? How can actors keep a communication between the others linked in the line? How can the next direction be made as the dance continues flowing in its line formation, keeping a sense of the society in the circle, but leading the society forward? I believe that this unspoken communication of dance can be made through the handhold, and dancing in this way can develop an actor's ability to communicate with fellow performers during live performance.

Hands to Lead

In these paintings the hands are only joined with very slight contact, often the fingers just touching. See how much leadership can be communicated in this handhold with as little connection as possible. It actually becomes easier for the follower to receive detailed information from the leader if the hands are lightly touching, rather than being held firmly. The tips of the fingers are able to reveal the intention of the leader, who can pass on signals by using a light touch.

Next in Line

Create exercises in couples with one person leading with a light touch – giving information on where to go in space, with what speed, even turning under the arms, stopping and starting motion. Place the arms in different positions – not simply by the side, but also raised in the air, and turning the partners under the arms. Practise the exercise until this method of leading and following is working well, and the leader is satisfied that the one person following is understanding every instruction by the use of the fingers on the hand.

Throw Some Shapes

From this free exploration, certain group shapes can be made, by extending into lines of three or more people. There are many different ways of making patterns with such a line, always moving the line forward, a free-flowing dance, and establishing moments when the leadership can change. These shapes made by a line of moving bodies have become known as *Farandole figures*, named after the folk dance found later in France, and descriptive names have been invented to match each variation.

Farandole Figure Examples: The Leader Makes the Choice

- Taking the group of dancers all around the room, in serpentine patterns, like a river flowing (*The Meander River*).

- Making one arch for the rest of the group to pass under (*Threading the Needle*).

- Making a line with all arms raised, through which the group can weave (*Church Windows*).

- Making a column of arches as each new leader turns to the partner joined and makes an arch (*Colonnade*).

- Taking the line of dancers into a circle and then coming out again (*Whirlpool*).

- Taking the line of dancers into the centre of a group circle and then the leader turning the second-in-line under the arms to pass over the entire line as the leader returns out of the circle (*L'Escargot – The Snail*).

The look of each of the patterns has determined what name has been attached to each figure, but even when a group of actors are completely conversant with the titles, the choice of the next move should be freely determined by the leader, and techniques should be found to let the handhold reveal the intention of what shape should be made. In practice, as soon as a leader hesitates and is physically unsure how to lead the line, the flow will stop and the line will buckle or break from the direction. The flow is visible through how the line responds to the leader who is able to communicate down the line.

The idea of making 'The Snail' is that the spiralling into the centre and then returning would make a pattern on the floor that from above would look like a snail shell. While making the floor pattern, however, the dancers must continue simply moving forward, and the leader must communicate while being on the move. This dance form requires the actor to continue the flow of motion while developing an awareness of the structures being made, knowing where everyone should be in this realm.

The Beat of the Feet

A painting on a wall cannot tell us what steps they made. Even the shapes of the bodies may not be physically possible when you try to reconstruct them with real live bodies. (The Nonsuch Dancers have explored several projects with the National Gallery in London, under the Dance in Art programme, looking at how the artist may be depicting dance, but even when it appears technically accurate, the actual physical realization from the painting is not always as easy as it looks!)

Steps are used to establish a metric pattern. The notion of a step can be defined as a transfer of the body weight. A step is simply taking the body weight from one foot to another, and the normal pattern when simply walking moves from one foot to another. Walking to different rhythms will attach the steps to specific beats, which may be evenly paced or stressing particular accents.

Saltarello is a technical term attached to pieces of Italian instrumental music from this period, and it is assumed that people would dance to this music. The term, from the Latin 'saltare', means 'to jump in the air', in effect to make little jumps from the floor, so it can be used to create steps of more variety than simply walking steps. In essence, making the human body leave the floor will change the activity of 'walking' to 'jumping'.

Jump to it!

Explore all ways you can jump from both feet, one foot, or between different feet. Continue walking and then decide in a split moment that you wish to jump. What preparation must you make before you make this jump? (Remember the safety issues connected to any kind of jumping: you need to bend the knees to prepare for a stretch through the body while achieving an elevation of the body, and, just as importantly, you need to bend the knees when landing to lessen the impact.) What different combinations can be made with jumping steps? Explore different jumping combinations that move from one leg to another, onto the same leg, or between both legs.

A Laban Dance approach analysing the transference of body weight will identify these as five possible jumps:

[2-2]
From standing on Two Legs to land back onto Two Legs
'two to two'

[2-1]
From Two Legs to land on One Leg
'two to one'

[1-1]
From One Leg to the Same Leg
'one to same'
(This is often called a hop – which is considered a type of jump in this system.)

[1-1]
Same to Another
'one to the other'
(This moves from one side to the other: left to right / right to left.)

[1-2]
From One Leg back to Two Legs
'one to two'

Saltarello Step Recipe

1 Play *saltarelli* music (lively rhythmic instrumental music) and create different sequences with little jumps around the room.

2 Create one ordered combination of the five different jumps.

3 Learn the sequence by thinking only of the jump sequence you have created, varying how it fits to the music, and going in different directions.

4 Once you have committed your sequence to physical memory, join with the group, as one whole circle.

5 Revolve the circle to the left now, with everyone continuing their own variation of jump-steps. Maintain your own pattern, even though others have a different sequence.

6 Now make a circle with one other person by joining both hands. Remember, you are a physical representation of a circle, even though you are only two people joined by both hands. Perform your version of the *saltarello* while being joined to this partner. Do not alter your jumping sequence, even if the actual distance you travel is reduced and the direction has to be modified to revolve the small circle to the left.

7 When you are both confidently performing your own combination, then release one of the hands. The person with the left hand free is now the leader. That person leads, and the follower must fall into step with the leader's sequence.

8 Return to the two-person circle by joining hands again, and return to your own sequence so they work together in the same musical structure.

9 Repeat (from *7*), with the other person leading with their left hand free.

10 Enlarge the group of people in the circle to groups of three, or four, or more. Whatever pattern the leader makes of the different jumps, the line must try to follow. This exercise requires the followers to be very aware of whatever the leader does, and if the leader alters his pattern, they should follow and adapt accordingly. This is a Feudal world – and whatever the leader does, the society must comply.

Modify this exercise without expending so much energy either as a leader or as a follower, making sure the steps are small – *saltarelli* does mean little jumps after all. Little jumps can be interspersed within the ordinary walking steps, rather than jumping continuously. Also, introduce the idea that the linked dancers in their own lines will use the dancing to meet others in the space, rather than only being concerned with the steps of the leader. Meet other groups in the space, as if you are continuing your usual daily business, as in the painting of the Siena scene. Don't lose the sense of the leader's physical presence, but try to present the idea that there is agreement in following the lead of this person at the head of the line. In improvised dance forms this is the illusion to be displayed to the onlookers: the 'effects of good government in a secure city' should occur without the controlling mechanism (the political power) being explicitly on view, and without the followers simply slavishly copying the person next to them, with their head down, focusing only on the task of jumping, but instead engaging with the world around them.

Metric Motion to Music

Now that music has been introduced, you may be one of those people who want to start to count the beats that fit the musical structure, that is, identify the 'metre'. Metre is a vital part of any lyrical art: to create poetry, to compose music, and to choreograph balanced patterns of body movement. The danger with counting in dance is that it can appear the most important element and may prevent other interactive elements being sensed by you as the actor. Metric rhythm is only one part of dance, and it must also be part of other rhythms if the dance is to stay part of the drama.

Steps and Circles Connect

Natural Sways

After such wild exploration of making patterns around the room and stepping with jumps, it is worth returning to the basic circle formation and placing these leadership techniques into a circle: moving in the same direction as a group, working together as you sway from side to side; continuing the sway for longer in one direction, and then returning back to where you were. Think of the flow of the circle moving the whole group in one direction, and then returning. The moment of change may occur at any point when the group decides communally, or a leader makes the choice. The aim is to make sure everyone moves together, and demonstrate that everyone is feeling the same momentum of the group sway.

Swaying with the Story

We can connect this to a storytelling structure, where the rhythm of the swaying is part of the narrative. It has been suggested that the medieval Icelandic sagas may have been told in a circle formation, with the swaying from side to side being connected to the telling of the story, and the drama of the scene being interpreted by the way the group would move in one direction and back again, creating a combined art form of chanting and swaying, given the name *sagna-dans*. You can explore this by telling an everyday saga – with someone beginning to describe 'something that happened to me while walking down the street one day'. This person also controls the swaying of the circle, always changing the direction of the circle when something new happens in the tale. Change leaders and let the images in the story influence the rhythm of the circle, the length of time of movement in one direction, the motion towards the forward left or backward right, and the stepping of the feet. This free exploration will need to become rooted into a musical form for the performance to be considered dance in the medieval period, and the steps will comply with particular poetic structures of the verse.

Carolling

Swaying in circles, with hands holding, and voices singing verses, has been classified as 'carols', and the activity of singing while dancing is called 'carolling' in the literature of this period. The idea of a carol as a Christmas tradition is rooted in this form of dance-song, although they were created for many other times of the year, including spring and summer. This historical connection between dancing and singing can establish patterns in an ordered musical rhythm, and this musical structure can introduce the basic step units as building blocks for organizing patterns of steps.

The value for the actor of learning circle dances is to consider how these three ways of communicating may combine:

- *The Organic Rhythm* and connection to rhythms in nature occurring as a change in energy – the natural flow of the movement.

- *The Narrative Rhythm* and connection to changes in direction as the story has something new to say – the punctuation of the phrasing selected by the storyteller to add meaning to the movement.

- *The Musical Rhythm* as a dance with a repetitive structure (maybe with verse and chorus) – the metric song form organizing the form.

In performance, you may emphasize one of these elements or try to find connections between them. The basic step patterns found in set choreographies may appear very rigid when first encountered as simple instructions, but different ways of expression can be found by considering the combined rhythm that these steps make.

Sway Steps

Swaying towards the left and then the right produces an underlying structure for circle dance. The medieval French word for swaying is actually applied to the circle dances which move from one side to the other, described in the technical term 'bransle' or *'branle'*, which the English will pronounce as 'brawl'. This word is also used to describe a fighting activity, 'brawling' in the street – and it is possible to see how the word allows a shared meaning in the two actions. As we fight we attack forward and retreat in defence, just as the dance sways between two directions. It helps to think that a move in the left-side direction in a circle is taking the body forward, rather than to the side and backwards when travelling to the right side. You will find that in groups learning circle dances, some people will inevitably go in the wrong direction – and a real brawling may occur!

The actor can use these dances to develop the skill of controlling where to place the weight in the body, and working within different structural forms.

Basic steps will be added to this swaying motion: to produce step units that move to the left and to the right. Once they have been learnt in a circle, they can be taken as step units for moving anywhere around the room. I encourage you to remember the connection to this circular spatial structure, so that you can always think that they are making a shape that involves other elements beyond simply the steps: the overall shape being made in the space, and the connection to others sharing this space.

The Step Units

(As interpreted in the Historical Dance Reconstructions with the Nonsuch Dancers DVD.)

Branle [b]

The sway step (*branle*) gets the body moving. It is a preparation for moving somewhere in space. The body does not move away from the place it is located, as you rock from side to side, so it allows you to focus on the person with whom you are dancing, to begin swaying together. Historically, the musicians would be required to take their lead from the dancers, so this step sets the pace. When it occurs at times during the dance it reaffirms the connection between partners. It is the opposite of a fighting brawl that is needed at this moment: a dancing-brawl shows the harmony between the dancers before they begin a new phrase. It may be interpreted with the rising of the heels, joining at the end.

Simple Step [s]

The French word 'simple' is found in the dance manuscripts of the dances in the Burgundian court in the fifteenth century. It is indeed the most simple thing we can do in dance: make one step to move the body. It is a simple step, and the English translation of 'single' is useful to indicate that it is only one step of one foot. The usual combination is two singles as a compound step: stepping left and then right.

Analysing Weight Transference During the Compound Single Step Unit [ss]

As the weight of the body is taken to one side, one foot can take all the body weight. Let the other foot move towards that side, but don't let it take any of the weight of the body. Now the sway begins to the right, and this right foot takes the weight, the left foot joins next to right foot, but it only rests on the floor. The resting foot is ready to become active on the next step and move to the side for a 'simple' to the other side. Each change of body weight is one step, so once you have stepped to the left with a 'single left' it must be followed by a step with the right. This is fairly obvious in a circle formation joined with the hands of the other dancers, as it feels balanced to go in one direction and then the other. When not in a circle formation, it is usual to use single steps to move in a forward direction. Remember that the step is one transference of weight, so if the other foot comes forward to join the foot side by its side, it will only rest on the floor so that it is ready to make the next step with the alternate foot.

Double Steps [d]

Double double, toil and trouble.

The Weird Sisters in Shakespeare's play about the medieval monarch Macbeth use the phrase 'double double'. They conjure up 'toil and trouble' dancing a circle dance around their cauldron. If we follow the idea that there is a mystical good and bad side in the way our circle is danced, these witches would probably be travelling counterclockwise, against the natural flow of our harmoniously revolving planets, and believing that their contrary pattern would stir up evil. They are chanting the dance steps out loud in rhythm.

Remember, then, that the swaying steps relate to the amount of time taken to move the body in one direction. It does not actually require the number of steps to be doubled, but rather double the amount of musical time needed to make the steps that would balance two lots of single-step units.

In this way, one double equates to two single steps (d = ss). To ensure there is time for the change of direction at the end of the double step, the step comprises three changes of weight made by stepping on alternate feet, and then a coming together following the same principle as the single steps, where the weight of the body is resting on the last stepping foot, with the other foot balanced by the side ready to make the next move.

Reprise [r]

This dance term means take a step back. Take back the space you have stepped into. In the sample choreographies, the reprise has the same musical value as a double, which is typical, so it may be interpreted as a double step in a backwards direction. However, it may also be interpreted as one step backwards taking the same amount of music. This has been chosen for the Basse Danse sample, as it suits the long dress of the lady and gives time for the connection to occur between the two dancers as they turn their bodies towards each other.

Reverence [R]

The Plantagenet Bending of the Knee

Re-read the speech used as a quotation to open this chapter. At this moment in Shakespeare's depiction of Plantagenet politics in 1398, King Richard II realizes that his position as ruler is being challenged. No longer is anyone bowing to him as king. It is visually clear because the habitual reverential gesture is now lacking. At a medieval court, a formal gesture of a 'bending' of the knee would show respect to the ruler. The evidence we have of dances from the French Basse Danse of Burgundy notes the importance of the gesture of the *Reverence* as a motion beginning the choreographies.

Reverence

To Reverence
is to show
Respect.
R
written at the start of every dance
it is a royal requirement

Respect
contains the physical action of looking
Spect
(From the Latin word Spectare)
To Look

Re-
(again)

Respect:
to look
and
look again

not a double take
nor a look of disdain
never an immoral look

but a deeper look
to show
respect

Laban Dance Dimensions During the Reverence

1 Standing upright to communicate a feeling of awe and adoration (*neutral stance*).

2 Move forward and upward to display the body and connect the upper body with the presence ahead (*upward and forward*).

3 Then release the body down into the floor, letting one leg move into the backward space (*downward and backward*).

4 Continue looking forward and with a sense of the upward dimension. In this way, you are showing your reverence to the presence while maintaining your own respectful dignity.

Dimension Discussion

When you have made your Reverence, where should you look?

Surely the most respectful thing would be to bow your head?

The actor may show complete humility by lowering the head low. However, the lowering of the head may make it appear as if you do not want to be there, or that the *Reverence* is being made only in fear of the ruler. The most honest version is to remain looking forward and maintaining eye contact: the interaction can then continue throughout the entire gesture until the moment the *Reverence* leads into the next move.

The ways of communicating subtleties in this gesture need to be explored in practice. The scene may require a particular interpretation by the actor, adding other gestures of the head, the eyes, the hands. These additional gestures may reveal that, although the action of obeisance is being made, it is being performed simply as a functional act, a requirement of habit and tradition, and the character is really feeling disdain and disrespect at the moment of bowing.

Costume Aesthetics

- Extend the foot backward to display either the length of the man's leg in his fine hosiery or the splendid fabric of the lady's skirt.

- Keep the upper body in an upright placement so the medieval headgear such as the hennin hat of the lady stays high and the high-cut tunic of the man hangs decently from the waist!

Technical Tips

The *Reverence* prepares you to dance.
It is a test of balance and poise.
It is always a beginning of a new interaction.
Don't ...
– let the knee of the leg touch the floor: the fabric of the clothing must stay clean, and following this gesture of reverence you will need to raise the body immediately and continue dancing;
Don't ...
– use the arms to balance as you lower: find the balance from the central core and use your arms freely to express the reason for your reverence through gesture;

Don't ...
– raise your arms to the side as you lower, or you may appear as a vampire rising from the grave;
Don't ...
– lean forward as your leg goes back, or you may appear as a superhero about to take flight!

Courtly Love Codes

Formal marriage arrangements were established between men and women of noble birth with the intention that a particular dynastic line would continue to rule the realm. For this reason, the image of a dancing male–female couple was important as a symbol of social stability. A partnered formation of one man dancing with one lady also allows an opportunity for social interaction during the activity, and courtly love traditions may have existed as a way for valiant knights to woo their ladies in the medieval realm.

Following the art of Courtly Love, the gentleman should employ the sequence of looking for and getting agreement from his partner before making any physical contact and beginning the dance. All three of the following actions must be included in the one gesture of showing reverence:

Visus (to look) – use your eyes to see with respect.
Loqui (to speak) – ask if your partner is willing to dance (if not verbally, then ask with your eyes).
Contactus (to touch) – then offer your hand and allow contact to be made.

If parts of this procedure are omitted, there is a risk of misunderstanding. This is a courtly code to prevent partners being grabbed or refused publicly. The result may be intensely dramatic – or indeed unfortunately comic!

Side by Side

The usual formation for courtly couple dance has the gentleman to the left of his lady. The reasons for this arrangement may include the following points:

- The gentleman may still be wearing his sword, usually on his left.

- The usual leading hand is the right, so the man leads his lady with his strong right hand.

- The man has his left hand free, so, in keeping with the ideas of leadership explored during the circle dance, he has the task of leading the couple. *Keep thinking of these dances as circle dances danced only with two people.*

The two people are joined together, so it is a shared responsibility to sense the shape of the dance.

Handhold Gestures while Dancing

There are a number of options for the handhold that joins a dancing couple, with pictorial evidence supporting a variety of positions.

I encourage a courtly handhold that allows the lady to have a feeling of having the 'upper hand'. The easiest way of producing this is for the lady to place her hand on top of the gentleman's hand, so that she can release herself and move away from the dance at any moment. In this way, the gentleman must treat her with respect and communicate the direction to be taken by lightly touching the palm of his partner.

The steering of the partner should be hidden underneath, and for this reason a low handhold is preferred. Try to communicate which of the different basic step units (*branles, singles, doubles, reprise*) should be made and in which direction. Even if the dance will be taught as a set choreography, it is a good idea to have experimented with how versatile this can be, and how aware the follower can be to the command in the handhold.

Keeping the Circle During Couple Dances

When reconstructing step sequences, it is tempting to discard the idea of circling patterns, and free choice, and only learn the dance line-by-line, move-by-move. Try to continue the 'active surrounding' technique, even when the communal circle is broken and the couple performs a Show Dance for onlookers outside the dance.

The Nonsuch Dance Reconstructions include samples of such couple dances with repeating step sequences. The musical structures depend on the number of steps in each sequence, but it is worth imagining that the performers are still controlling the music, even if the music is recorded. The interactive connection with another performer creates other spatial structures within the general form of the dance, presented by where the steps take the body.

Comparisons Between *Basse Danse* and *Estampie* Reconstructed Spatial Forms

The dances are short choreographies, but require the actors to develop a skill of learning a number of different step patterns as part of an overall structure. Understanding the basic musical structure of each dance will help this in the beginning. The aim is for the dance to be experienced as a physical form occurring with a relationship to the other dancing partner. Consider the space where it is being performed and those who are observing the activity, and how a different feeling is experienced by the partners and the onlookers with a different surrounding of the space.

Nonsuch Dance Reconstruction (1) French Basse Danse – *La Dame*

One of many Basse Danse sequences written on a blank page in a Catholicon printed in Venice in 1497, now in the library of Salisbury Cathedral.

Reconstruction: Nonsuch Dances from the Courts of Europe, Volume 1.

Performed by one couple as a processional dance.

The steps do not leave the floor, as in the *saltarello*, but are executed with contact to the ground, which may be one interpretation of the title of these types of dances as '*basse*', meaning low.

[R] The *Reverence* is made facing forward – possibly towards a royal presence.

[b] The *branle* step punctuates the movement, allowing rhythmic connection between the partners. Later in the dance, this *branle* step will allow the couple to look from side to side with the swaying – maybe as a moment of privacy or to connect with onlookers at the side.

[ss] The *single steps* are taken forward and establish the pace and direction of the next section in the dance.

[d:r] *Double reprise combinations*: the number of doubles and reprise steps in basse danse choreographies varies, but always use odd numbers. Because of this rule, the double-step sequence begins with the left foot [L], and the first reprise step of each sequence goes backwards on the right [R].

The turning of the body during the reprise allows facing towards partners and then to the sides.

The actors need to consider the feelings that can be attached to different lyrical movement structures of long, short and medium phrases:

Long (3:3) = ddd: rrr = *LRL: RLR*
Short (1:1) = d:r = *L:R*
Medium (3:1) = ddd:r = *LRL: R*

The performers need to develop a spatial awareness of where the sequence of *doubles* and *reprise* will place the couple in the room for the swaying *branle* step. This step is both a full stop at the end of one lyrical phrase, and the preparation for the next, almost as a breath taken before speaking.

Circle Conversion: Circling Clockwise Becomes the Anticlockwise Line of Dance

Clockwise direction was established for circle dance. As couples joined together, evidence suggests that they danced anticlockwise around the room. This could develop from the formation of a medieval procession, when couples lined up behind each other and moved forward to meet a royal presence positioned at the front and then moved away, still wanting to travel forwards. It is easier for the man to sweep the lady forward with her long dress, as he can move backwards slightly to remain at her side. Now the man is closest to the centre of the room, and they can both process forward. Other couples would then all follow the leaders, and this would make a track around the room travelling anticlockwise. This conversion of the travelling of couples to an anticlockwise track becomes the standard way of dancing around the room as couples, and later will be given the technical term 'Line of Dance'.

The Basse Danse is a processional dance, so this same formation could be made, with each couple parading around the room. Being closer to the centre of the room, the man may find he has to take smaller steps to ensure that his lady can keep in step on the outside of the circle.

Nonsuch Dance Reconstruction (2)
Royal Estampie – *La Quinte Estampie Real*

From a collection of instrumental music entitled 'estampie' which implies that this is dance music performed for royal occasions between the twelfth and fourteenth centuries.

Reconstruction: Nonsuch Dances from the Courts of Europe, Volume 1.

The Estampie has been imagined as a figured dance, so that different patterns are made by where the steps are placed on the floor, both giving a different view of the dancing bodies to any onlookers and evoking different feelings to the performers. Consider how the steps towards and away from the partners create different figures of leaving and returning that communicate different feelings between the dancers.

The music is divided into sections called *puncta* – each of these phrases is repeated with two musical endings (open ending *apertum*, and closed ending *clausum*). This means that each *punctum* may have a different number of musical beats and therefore a different number of steps. Choreographies have been created to match the musical structures.

Punctum 1 (ssd): forward and backward to acknowledge the presence.

Punctum 2 (dssd): initially displayed to the front, moving to the left side in the room, then upon returning they face each other, moving to their own left side and back to meet face to face.

Punctum 3 (ssdss): the dancers make a small circle using a handhold and stepping around the circumference.

Punctum 4 (5s d): a variation of five walking steps to move apart before joining together.

Summary: Circling the Space

The historical period in this chapter has allowed a consideration of how society may dance as one communal group, all being part of a circle. Smaller groups would be able to dance differently under different leaders, while sharing the space and finding techniques with contact through eyes and hands to communicate the physical intention of their lines. The smallest group of two, a dancing couple, can begin by considering how they circle the space, making a procession around the room, and also taking the steps in different directions but remaining as a joined partnership. The actors require skills of leading, following and developing spatial awareness of the patterns being made by the whole body in relation to the partners, the onlookers, the musical structures and the architecture of the room. These are the building bricks to give dance a structure.

Further Research Springboard

- Text:
  - Dante's *Inferno* and the Circles of Hell, as types of characters dancing together.
  - The Dance of Death idea in medieval miracle plays as all are characters following the social hierarchical chain.
  - The history of the figures from the Plantagenet dynasty: inspiring Shakespeare's history plays, including the War of the Roses.
- Image:
  - Angelic dance depicted in Gothic churches, cathedrals and frescos such as Giotto and Fra Angelico.
  - Social dance depicted in the mural *The Effects of Good Government in the Secure City*, Palazza Publico, Siena, by Ambrogio Lorenzetti (c. 1290–1348).
- Music:
  - Carol singing and dancing: *Sumer is Icumen In* of England.
  - Estampie instrumental dances of France.
  - Saltarelli tunes of Italy.
  - Reconstructions from Basse Danse manuscripts of France and Spain.

3
ITALIAN BALLS:
RENAISSANCE RHYTHMS

What's he that follows there, that would not dance?

JULIET ASKS THE NURSE ABOUT ROMEO
AFTER THE CAPULET BALL SCENE,
SHAKESPEARE'S *ROMEO AND JULIET*,
ACT I, SCENE 5

Within the Time Frame

- In the fifteenth century, Italian courts such as Florence and Siena were established as dukedoms with ruling families, such as the House of Medici.

- Classical ideas influenced a new approach to artistic production that came to be considered a cultural rebirth: the Renaissance.

- An identifiable style of art in painting, sculpture, architecture and poetry was established with shared production techniques.

- Music and dance were connected to these specific courts, employing their own dancing masters, who produced detailed dance treatises.

- Festivals were created to display the wealth and culture of the courts, employing figures such as Leonardo da Vinci.

An Actor Prepares to …

- Place dance in a social context of a court, considering formal requirements and ways to interact socially while dancing set patterns.

- Make aesthetic choices in movement to emphasize the fashionable clothing.

- Create dance structures related to architectural principles of the performance space.

- Learn the skills noted by the dancing masters as ways to become physically graceful while moving.

- Interpret the Historical Dance terminology of 'measure' to create dramatic scenarios within choreographies.

- Find a style for moving the body, combining the overall posture with specific step patterns.

- Alternate between different rhythms in one choreography.

- Hold a plan of the overall dance and the rhythmical changes in mind while physically performing in the present.

- Develop memory of dance sequences.

- Admire and be admired while dancing.

Foot it Girls!

Take Shakespeare's *Romeo and Juliet.* The two lovers meet during a dance scene. The tragic drama begins at this moment when Romeo sees Juliet dancing, and his newly felt desire immediately replaces his former love for Rosaline. Had Juliet not danced when she did, then Romeo may not have noticed her. Immediately following the dance, Romeo feels compelled to speak directly to Juliet, and both characters express intense emotions.

The dance scene is pivotal in this play as it allows the story to develop, bringing a large number of the characters together to establish the social context of the drama. I am calling this a 'dance scene' because it is not only the display of the dancing that is important, but also what happens in and around this activity. The dance has a particular part to play in the dramatic structure, contributing both to the narrative and character development. The most senior character speaks to initiate the dancing: Capulet, the head of the family and father of Juliet, will not allow any of his guests to 'deny to dance'. He invites those who have arrived masked 'in visors', maybe addressing the disguised characters of Mercutio, Benvolio and Romeo. It is possible in this case to suggest that all the actors could perform the first dance onstage at this moment, although Romeo is later identified as the person 'that would not dance'.

There are many options for when dance occurs, maybe as one short dance to set up the scene, a continuous dance running throughout the scene, or a sequence of different dances. Dancing could occur immediately following Capulet's command to 'foot it, girls!'. At the end of his speech, Capulet invites his similarly aged relative to sit and watch. Dancing occurs as the central activity, preoccupying each character in their own way.

Romeo is watching the dancing so intently that he is oblivious to the fact that Tybalt has seen through his masked disguise. Tybalt then reveals Romeo's identity to Capulet. Whichever way we look at it, Romeo should not have been there. He was not invited to be at the occasion, he should not have witnessed the dance, and he breaks the social rules by being present.

Tybalt wants to confront Romeo and have him removed from the occasion, but Capulet overrules this, letting the festivities continue uninterrupted. Indeed Romeo's focus remains fixed entirely on Juliet, and when he speaks his thoughts, he can only praise Juliet's beauty, being clearly impressed by her moving body. Juliet is 'enriching' the arm of another 'knight', which could imply that Juliet was still connected physically to a partner in a dance.

Romeo decides to make his move when the 'measure' is done, and at an opportune moment, Romeo takes Juliet's hand, speaks to her and they eventually kiss. To ensure that this appears as a private exchange, it is possible that the other guests would continue dancing in the background.

The Prologue to Shakespeare's *Romeo and Juliet* tells us that the scene is set in 'fair Verona', and the old Italian story upon which the Shakespeare play is based was known to have been of a much earlier period than Elizabethan England, presenting political structures of feuding families that were in existence in Italy during the fourteenth and fifteenth centuries. The original production of this play may not have made any obvious reference to this specific earlier period, as indeed many productions since have not needed to either. However, an historical imagining of this general time period that has been called the *Italian Renaissance* does offer insight into how dance could be viewed as a vital part of society, how one style of movement can be used to unify a group, how drama can occur in the structure of a patterned ordered formal dance, and how personal interpretation can be performed within such a formal structure. This knowledge of different rhythms can deepen our understanding of how the scene itself is structured, and how the dance can be woven into the fabric of the play, and used as part of the actor's craft of communicating drama through organized movement.

Although we now use the word *Renaissance* to define this period, the word was not used at the time. The French word, meaning 'rebirth', was coined by the art historian Jules Michelet in 1855 to identify a break from the medieval period and signify the return of classical ideas to inspire art and culture.

The Italian Renaissance dancing masters reimagined classical principles to develop a dance style that used rhythmic structures complying with mathematical musical analysis and with spatial patterning connected to the theory of artificially arranged perspective in architecture. Narrative and character were inspired by the ancient myths of gods and goddesses, but with attention on how the human body could be refined by movement training, interacting in a shared noble style. In particular, choreographies were created, especially for noble families to display their grandeur. The fictional ball at the House of Capulet may be imagined as such an occasion.

Renaissance Italy was actually made up of principalities and dukedoms, with noble houses gathered politically under each ruler. Festivities displayed the power of each prince or duke, and families used organized occasions to celebrate new alliances, both in war and love, celebrating peace treaties and weddings, making links between other noble families, ruling duchies and royal courts of other European countries. We can hypothesize that, had Romeo not attended the Capulet ball, Juliet would have married County Paris and this arrangement would have strengthened the family's link directly to the Prince. Capulet invites Paris to woo his daughter in the hope of forming a future alliance, and a ball would be a very possible place to do this.

Dance was a major part of all such formal occasions. The dance scene in *Romeo and Juliet* occurs as part of a family feast, with invited guests selected because of their alliance to the Capulet family. Such an occasion would enable a family to parade their most prized possessions: daughters of the family, who would be part of patriarchal negotiations to form new alliances between families, with the intention of continuing the dynasty and enhancing their political power. These young ladies would have been instructed in how to dance and move gracefully, in preparation for joining their noble partners at such occasions. If Juliet had lived in the Italian Renaissance she would have received this type of dance instruction.

Dance in this period was considered as the art of *misura,* which we can translate as 'measure' – measuring both time and space with the movement of the body. The training required instruction from dancing masters who would be employed by the noble families, becoming well established as part of the household. Theatrical spectacles included dance performance involving display and disguise. Italian dances called *maschera* imply elements of 'masquerading' and 'masking'. These elements have already been indentified as appearing in the dance scene in *Romeo and Juliet*, and the word 'measure' in Shakespeare may sometimes refer to the overall concept of dance, rather than a specific dance.

The following exercises consider how historical evidence can reconstruct a physical interpretation of Italian Renaissance dance forms, with the aim of showing what particular elements were valued in the dance practice of the time.

So how would a young girl like Juliet have danced in the Italian Renaissance?

- What skills would she have needed to learn?

- What things would the family dancing master have reminded her to think of along the way?

- Maybe her mother would have had a similar dance training and passed on her instruction?

- What knowledge would the Nurse have had now from her years of experience?

- As a servant to the household, the Nurse herself may not have danced the noble dances, but she would have at least watched many such occasions.

- Dances would have been performed at all celebrations – Juliet's father mentions the wedding celebrations of 30 years earlier, the 'nuptials of Lucentio', when he wore a mask and danced the steps.

- How can the art of dance be considered noble, and how can this movement ensure that the person appears attractive to those with whom they are dancing and to the onlookers of the event?

Although these are still social dances, they are also created as works of art to impress those looking on – be they a proud father or a secret lover.

Dance Treatises: Historical Notes

Many noble houses, such as those of the Sforza family, paid their dancing masters well. We have full titles for some of these dancing masters from the fifteenth century, such as Domenico of Ferrara or Domenico of Piacenza, and his disciples Antonio Cornazano and Guglielmo Ebreo da Pesaro. It is likely that this same Guglielmo Ebreo, whose name translates literally as 'William the Jew', changed his name to Giovanni Ambrosio when, in order to continue as part of the noble household, he was required to convert to Christianity. Dance instruction from these masters is preserved in collections of treatises, probably given as gifts to the noble households for whom they worked.

Friendly Advice

Their names may sound rather grand, but I think it is best to get to know them simply as Dom, Tony and Will. They are like friends offering their advice on how to make sure you look good while dancing. The written accounts from our three friends suggest a shared style, but even with the written descriptions we have, there are issues of interpretation, and gaps that will need to be filled by considering other poetic descriptions and depictions in the art from the period. The Italian Renaissance is a prolific period in the history of art, and much of the paintings and architecture can be great inspiration for the look and feel of the period. Words, pictures and physical practice need to combine.

Exploring the Graces of Dance

Above all, in this period, dance should be graceful: full of many graces. The treatises all discuss similar qualities in dance practice that must be combined together to make the perfect performance in the art of dance, uniting to give the visual appearance of nobility and refinement. Specifically for the actor working in the studio, I have selected some of the main ideas from these treatises that enable a physical style to be explored immediately. Alongside the terminology, I have listed a selection of poetic and descriptive words inspired by their writings that can be interpreted using a Laban Dance approach to produce instructions to achieve the physical embodiment of these concepts.

Extreme Measures

The main thing to bear in mind is that the writers all warn against going to extremes. The treatises warn their noble readers against doing too much or too little in practice – rather, maintain a *mean of your movement*. To find this 'mean' it is necessary to discover the middle balance between the two extremes. You may go to the extremes first – both ends of the scale – doing too much of each element so it is grotesquely comic, and then doing so little that it is not even perceivable by an observer. Then attempt to find the balance between the two states.

Pictorial Evidence

Large collections of art, of paintings, sculpture and artefacts chosen to represent the Italian Renaissance are on display in our national art galleries. However, we can only find one single small visual illustration amongst our collection of dance treatises. In the 1463 treatise entitled *On the Practice of Dancing*, attributed to Guglielmo Ebreo, there appears a picture depicting one man in the centre with a lady on either side, with their inside arms linked by their fingers, lifted from the elbow. We assume that the man at the side playing a harp is accompanying the trio, which may imply that the three people are dancing together.

Clothing: High Legs and Long Skirts

The clothing they are wearing is in keeping with the fashion of the day. The man wears a short tunic that exposes the length of his legs: every step the man makes will be on show for all to see. The long trains of the ladies' dresses are draped on the floor, presenting potential hazards of tripping-up or partners stepping on the hem. Her stepping legs may not be scrutinized as much, but she will need to display skill controlling this flowing dress as she dances.

Stepping Together

In the treatise, there are descriptions of dances for three dancers, although there are also other dances requiring other numbers of dancers and combinations of men and women. The three dancers in the illustration are looking forward. All three have their right foot forward so this evidence can be used to support the rule that all dancers will use the same footing when dancing the same sequence of steps together. Unless told otherwise, dancers will begin stepping together and then alternate only as the choreography requires. The uniformity of all stepping together does affirm the feeling of solidarity in the group, and presents a visual symbol of a unified society.

Ruling Lines

As to the placement of the feet, the toes seem to be pointing fairly straight forward. From this evidence we can support an idea of keeping the feet in parallel position whenever possible, in both moments of rest and during the dance. We will maintain this as the standard for this technique, and connect this idea to the designs for the floors of Renaissance palaces, with the tiles producing lines to follow, and architectural plans making the perspective clear. The structures of the choreographies will depend on the precise placement of the bodies in space to produce the best perspective for the onlooker.

Linking Handholds

What does appear peculiar in the treatise illustration is the way that the arms are placed and the hands are joined. The man has both his hands raised, with his elbows bent. His hands link to each lady on either side with their little fingers wrapped around his. The written descriptions only refer simply to the taking of hands, with no further explanations of how to do this. The two ladies do have their arms bent in, seemingly resting on their bodies, which may imply a resting position. All three are facing forwards, focusing on the presence watching this performance; in this way it could be the end of the sequence. If this is a final position, however, then the hands of the harpist are still playing music at this moment, and this should remind us that the art of dance is always flowing continuously, right through to the final bow. So, whether this is a position to start or end the dance, or a momentary position midway through the dance, where partners join hands, in practical terms we always have to consider how to keep moving physically between such positions. Dance is a part of the wider social interaction at these Renaissance festivities, so we must always consider how to move into this particular mode of dance performance and then how to move from the completed dance into ordinary pedestrian movement while maintaining the noble style.

   When choreographies are reconstructed a decision will need to be made as to how to interpret the simple phrase 'take hands'. We will need to consider what is most appropriate for the context and the actors involved, and to comply with the overall aesthetic style. Like Old Capulet, I invite you to explore through practice the actual words of the historical dance masters to discover the 'noble disposition' identified with the Italian Renaissance.

Movimento Corporeo: Graceful Body Motion

The dancing master Giovanni Ambrosio writes a chapter in his treatise directed specifically to the ladies. There are many instructions about graceful movement such as:

If you want to delight in dancing, then have more modesty than the men ...

Hold your body nobly, move your feet with agility and let your arms make perfectly formed gestures ...

Don't be arrogant or flirtatious with your eyes: look down modestly at the floor but don't drop your head: stay upright, moving both gracefully and moderately.

(Peggy Dixon Collection, Paris Bibliotheque Nationale facsimile, f. Ital. 476. Book 1)

Combining Many Graces

Walking in the Air

Technical Terms: *aire / aere / airosa / ondeggiare*
Poetic Interpretation: airy / lightness / lift / expansion / breath / soft-rising
Laban Dance: light / suspended / gliding / floating

- Allow the upper carriage to be lifted and the shoulders to feel suspended.

- Use this elevation of the upper carriage to feel ennobled.

- Imagine the entire body filling with air and keep suspended as you move forward.

- Express an open freedom and gentle flow as you move around the space.

- Allow this air-like quality in the body to produce an elevation in the steps you make, so once you have raised up your body you can remain suspended as you step forward on the toes of the feet.

- Each step adds a feeling of rise, and then lower through the floor, connecting with the breath.

Shading the Steps

Technical terms: *maniera / campeggiare / agilitade*
Poetic interpretation: adding style / display / shading / adornment
Laban Dance: body part opposition / upper body motion / counter-tension

- Using the carriage of the upper body to give a presentational style to each step.

- Upper body carriage: letting the shoulders move freely, from neutral position to one forward with one backward, alternating sides, with ribs lifted.

- Allowing one side of the body to move forward with each step (explore moving with the same side as the stepping foot and then the opposing side).

- Maintaining this adornment throughout each whole step (for example, do one shoulder-shading for the entire *doppio* double step, rather than on each change of foot).

- Be careful you do not raise the shoulders – only move them forward and backward.

The Agile Body with the Dancing Spirit

Technical terms: *agilitade and fantasmata*
Poetic interpretation: alert imagination
Laban Dance: focus in space / awake mode

- Make agile and nimble movements as you move around the space.

- Physical quickness and alertness.

- Reacting to those around you.

- Staying in the moment with stillness and focus, followed by suddenly taking off with zestful energy 'like a hungry falcon taking flight'.

The Body in Motion: Recalling Emotional Changes in Time and Space

Rhythm

Misura – Measure

There are four types of measure identified by the Italian Renaissance dancing masters.
In order of increasing speed, these are:

bassadanza   (given the title 'The Queen of Measures')
quadernaria   (in which one note is one-sixth shorter)
saltarello   (two-sixths or one-third shorter)
piva   (three-sixths or one half shorter)

The Ladders of Misura

Developed from Antonio Cornazano, *The Art of Dancing*, 1455.

Since *misura* connects to the art of metre in music, it is possible to approach the system mathematically, analysing the timing of the steps. To begin with, however, the idea will be that these are imagined simply as different gear shifts, which allow the actor to experience different modes of moving. The most important thing for the actor is to think of these as changes of emotion, and find particular personal reasons why a new speed is used at a particular moment in the dance.

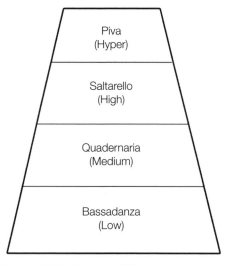

Figure 3.1 Mathematical Pyramid

Bassadanza – like the French term *Basse Danse* – has the idea of being low to the ground. Being the Queen of Measures, let it glide along the floor, elegantly and sustained.

Quadernaria – a four-square feeling – not necessarily with a count of four, but more in keeping with the idea of moving in an ordered system, having a military feel, with angles and direct lines.

Saltarello – this general term of leaving the floor with a jump can be given a particular place in this measured system: it is so light that you can skim above the surface, and move quickly, so the little jumping is caused by the propelling energy that moves you forward.

Piva – the word relates to the bagpipes played by the Italian shepherds – probably in a wild and raucous fashion. In this measure system it is the most wild, being fast and furious.

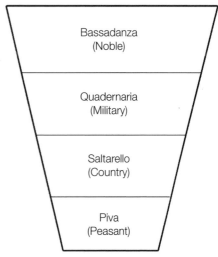

Figure 3.2 Hierarchical Measure

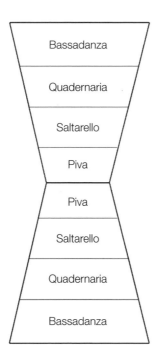

Figure 3.3 Hourglass Measure

The idea of different modes can relate back to the ancient ideas of planetary motion, and changes in quality of movement by how time and space are used while dancing. The Ladders of Misura may be developed to correspond to our previous spherical model for movement modes.

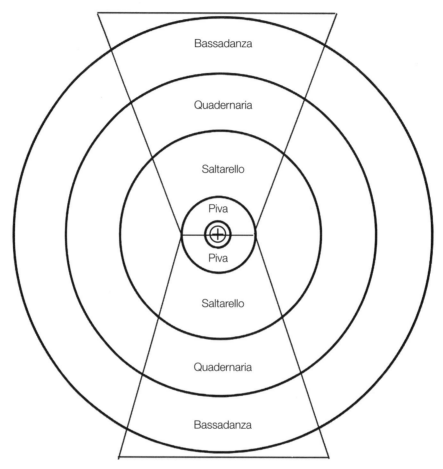

Figure 3.4 Spherical Measures

Humanist Measures

These four states can be explored in a fun way by establishing a basic slow walk around the studio, and creating the faster measures one by one. Once these are established, change between the different rhythms when something happens in the studio – when you meet someone, when you see something, as you remember something, or decide to move to a particular place in the space. The fastest step, the *piva*, should be challenging, although be careful that you can stop and control yourself as others will be moving at different paces in the room. The *bassadanza* will also need a different form of control. Only then think of the names of the measures. Explore what it feels like to move in sequence up and down the measure scale, from one extreme to the other, and out of sequence – such as from lively *saltarello* to grave *bassadanza* to wild *piva* to solid *quadernaria* – and other combinations that surprise you by not knowing what will come next. It is worth considering other terms to attach to the four measures that relate to the feelings you have while performing them, and how you might remember such modes.

The feet will need to find a particular step to match each of these rhythms, although the treatises often do not specify this amount of detail. The measure needs to govern how the body is moving, and this then determines how the feet may move.

Dividing Space

concordantia di terreno / compartimento di terreno / partire del terreno

- How the performer divides the space of the floor while dancing.
- Arranging the space in your mind before setting out.
- Adjusting your steps to fit the space to arrive at the correct place and with your partner.
- Adapting the length of the steps (in speed or rhythm) to fit the room.

Things to Consider

- Architecture of the space.
- The status in the space – and whether a powerful presence has been identified.
- Other people in the space – moving in the dance, static for moments of the dance, or observing.
- The perspective and how the dance would appear from different viewpoints.
- Structures being made in the space.
- Lines on the floor for the patterns to follow.
- Relationship to your partner(s) and connections between the moving bodies – imagine this as magnetism, with a feeling of moving between attraction and repulsion between the partners as you move towards or away.

Memory (*Memoria*)

It is an obvious thing to state that it is necessary to remember the steps in a dance. However, the inclusion of this term in the Italian Renaissance treatises emphasizes memory as a very physical activity. All these ideas of how to dance with this particular graceful style need to be united as one experience and recalled together. It implies that the individual needs to employ an awareness to capture as much of this ephemeral art in the practice, so that all these qualities exist together in performance as a complete work of art.

Add Grace to the Execution of Dance Steps

The basic units remain the same, although they are given Italian terminology and combine all the above stylistic qualities. It is important that the style pervades every move, so that it appears cohesive, calm and connected.

Riverenza / Riverentia (R): The Reverence

We have explored the *reverence* in detail in the previous chapter – and in some ways there are no major changes that need to be made to the outward form of this Italian equivalent, the *riverenza*. It is worth reminding yourself of the meaning of this gesture and the many things which need to connect in one move. The actor may need to execute a different way of performing the move, to make it appear an expression of personal grace rather than feudal subservience.

Lift up and connect with the 'air' quality before releasing into the floor, allowing one leg to move into the backward space. Keep the upright suspension in the body, and avoid the arms lifting and the head sinking. Try to keep the head upright even when the eyes may look towards the floor. There are many moments now in these choreographies where a *riverenza* must be made, so it is part of the language of the actual dance, in addition to being something that begins and ends the entire dance. Because of this, the the 'aere' element is vital, as it is felt as a moment of breath, ready to move onto the next phrase in the choreography. When the *riverenza* is found in the sequence of the dance, the graceful quality should make it more like a midway pause, a breathing comma, rather than a finite full stop.

From paintings, it is clear that the hands are so important to signify the link between dancers. The hands of partners may join on the reverence. One interpretation uses the idea of joining '*palm to palm*', rather as Juliet will say '*like Holy Palmer's Kiss*', touching palms and remaining linked as the lowering takes place. This allows a more intimate physical connection between the two performers.

Travelling Steps

The left foot will continue to be assumed to be the first foot to begin each step pattern, unless an instruction is given to do otherwise. The choreographies in these treatises are written in long hand, describing the sequence in order, and more often than not the stepping simply alternates from one foot to the other, with moments of pause where the body suspends before taking the next step.

Sempio (s): The Single Step

With one transference of weight of the body on each step, adding *maniera* to each step, bringing the other foot to close. An 'open' single step does not close the foot, but remains suspended behind: it is an artistic choice in some choreographies to emphasize the flowing on the step, but the performer must be careful that this does not appear as someone stepping with a limp! The conscientious use of the vertical elevation can prevent this.

Doppio (d): The Double Step

With three steps transferring the body weight, rise on the first step, and remain in the suspended elevated position for the next two steps, before lowering as the leg comes to rest at the side of the foot. To achieve the suspension when the feet close, the heels may barely touch the floor. The shoulder adornment should last for the whole duration of the *doppio*, not as a series of shoulder movements made on each change of foot, nor as something that only begins the step and is then forgotten. This is a test for keeping the graceful carriage of the body throughout the whole step.

Continentia (Plural: *Continentie*) (c)

Small steps, often occurring in pairs, and can be taken to each side, or sometimes to one side only.

Ripresa (Plural: *Ripreses*) (r)

The side steps – they are interpreted as single steps, maybe with a feeling of pulling back in space.

Volta Tonda (vt): The Turning Step (vt = ssr)

Meaning simply to turn around, sometimes the dance specifies that it comprises two singles beginning on the right, with a *ripresa* to the right. You may be precise about the placement of these steps, and suggest a quarter turn on each single and a half turn for the final turning *ripresa*, to conclude facing the direction where the step began.

Movimento (m): The Mystery Move

At times in the choreography the instruction asks the dancers to make a *movimento*. Simply meaning a move or a gesture, this could be physically interpreted in many ways, and the moment in the dance may suggest a particular way of making this with a particular dynamic: such as more sudden and spikey, or more sustained and gentle. Of course it is exciting to be presented with an opportunity to give your own interpretation within the dance. However, whatever actual move is chosen as a gesture, it should feel to belong to the overall style of the period movement. This is an ideal opportunity to bring together all the graceful elements the dancing masters wanted to combine in the body while dancing.

What is involved in a *movimento*?

- It is a gesture made by the individual, often as a solo action by one dancer to then be repeated by others in the dance.
- The dancer is saying something with the gesture at this point in the choreography.
- The dancer is communicating to someone in the dance before continuing dancing with them.
- The dancer is not moving from the place, being rooted in one spot.

Take on board the advice from Domenico:

> Appear as a gondola, being propelled smoothly through calm waves.
> (*NHD Peggy Dixon Collection, translated from Paris Bibliotheque Nationale, f. Ital. 972. chapter 3*)

Make a rise and fall of the body in the *movimento*, with the impetus coming from underneath the heels of the feet, as if the gondola were moved by waves. The body, still filled with air, should feel light and the shoulders now released in this elevated position, so that they can adorn the move with an airy sway backwards and forwards, letting one shoulder move subtly backward first. After a while, you may notice that the move has become a rise and fall of the shoulders – this is a habitual error – this 'shimmy shake' clearly contradicts the idea of grace we are trying to achieve. The gesture is not made with the shoulders; they are only a shading to the rise of the heels, caused by the calm sea flowing underneath and lifting the body.

Once you have mastered your version of a *movimento*, as a momentary gesture in the flow of the dance, then we can begin the movements that take the body into different dimensions and consider choreographed patterns.

Learning Reconstructed Dances

While learning the reconstructed dances, consider how different approaches can be used to make the dance dramatic.

Expressive Dance

Suggest images to relate to the qualities identified in this style of moving, and set out to discover a feeling of being connected with other people, imagining invisible threads still in existence as you move away or close to each other.

Historical Dance

The steps are given, but the exact floor patterning must be discovered as you step it out in practice.

Laban Dance

This style is predominantly determined by one established weight quality (*air*). Changes in the choreography relate to *space* (distance between the partners) and *time* (whether the steps remain in the sustained flow, or change suddenly).

Consider how the following elements create the style:

- vertical axis
- dynamics: spatial rhythms
- feet action: rise and fall
- upper body carriage
- shoulder adornment

Show Dance

Consider situations that would be relevant to the number of dancers and their organized formation. Suggested narratives:

- Lovers meeting for the first time.
- A secret meeting on the dance floor.
- Moving from private to public space.
- The wedding dance.

Choreographies Using One Misura: Bassadanza

Some dances are created to match music of only one of the *misura*. The *bassadanza* is the slowest rhythm. This trains the actor to keep a sustained flow in the dance, moving into the various patterns seamlessly and ensuring that the phrasing is continuous. The drama of the dance can be found in the spatial patterning attached to the step sequences.

Nonsuch Dance Reconstruction (3)
Italian *Bassadanza* for a Couple – *Alexandresca*

Reconstruction: Nonsuch Dances from the Court of Europe, Volume 2, Guglielmo Ebreo.

Two people are connected magnetically, beginning the dance following each other, keeping the attraction even when they separate, spiralling in to meet with passion, and ending formally side by side. The slow speed of the dance requires the dancers to glide and feel suspended, in particular with the steps to either side. The partners stay connected even when not able to look directly at each other, having moments where they turn to face, and using peripheral vision to match their patterning on the floor when they make a 'figure of 8' together, which must also pass through the established central point. This reconstruction allows the dancers to separate out as far as is possible, so that the moment when they turn back suddenly to face each other has more impact with such a distance between them. The reverence keeps this connection from afar, but the desire to get closer to each other again pulls the partners together, as they are drawn closer to each other, spiralling. The only moment of contact uses a handhold with just the little fingers joined, and as they return to standing, the formal courtly handhold is reinstated. This could be imagined as a dance where two lovers meet for the first time, maybe a secret meeting, resisting communicating all their private thoughts to each other, and feeling guarded in a public space.

Nonsuch Dance Reconstruction (4)
Italian *Bassadanza* for Three – *Pellegrina*

Reconstruction: Nonsuch Dances from the Court of Europe, Volume 2, Guglielmo Ebreo.

This reconstruction begins by giving focus to the man in the middle, as he steps into line between the two ladies. Throughout the choreography he is required to move his attention between both of the ladies, almost as a Romeo figure with fluctuating passions. To respect both ladies, the gesture of Reverence must give equal attention to both partners. He is placed in a triangular formation, joining hands with one lady as the other turns her back to revolve on her own track, before he repeats this with the other lady. A connection remains between the three dancers even when they separate, and this energy can be imagined being projected through their backs, so that the sudden moment of turning to face again exposes the desire to stay connected. The physical coming together requires the skill of maintaining the *bassadanza* measure while dividing the floor space with the steps, to present the final image of three people linked harmoniously. This choreography can be done with groups of three dancers lined up behind each other, so that dancers pass other dancers when separating out from their own partners. This also requires the actors to agree on the placements on the floor to make the lines straight and the patterns geometrically exact. Dancing as one group in organized lines can give the impression of one whole family exuding its 'house style' with unified *maniera*.

Choreographies Using a Variety of Misura: Balli

The choreographies with changes of rhythm require the actor to consider dramatic reasons for why the body will move into a different dynamic at certain moments in the dance.

Nonsuch Dance Reconstruction (5)
Italian *Ballo* for a Couple – *Rostibolly Gioisa*

Reconstruction: Nonsuch Dances from the Court of Europe, Volume 2, Domenico da Ferrara.

The word *gioisa* implies a 'joyful' occasion, and *rosti bolli* means 'roasted' and 'boiled'. Wedding banquets in this period would alternate courses between roasted and boiled meats, so maybe the title connects the dance to a feasting occasion. Dancing masters organized such celebrations; for example, Guglielmo was master at the Milan wedding of Eleanora d'Aragona to the Duke of Bari in 1465.

This dance can be imagined as depicting the ritual of marriage. A *ballo* by definition will include different *misura* rhythms. This dance begins in slow *bassadanza* in keeping with the charged intensity between the two lovers, maybe relating to the idea of things hotting up, in a roasting and boiling way! The man and lady have moments to make their own vows to each other at the beginning, before creating patterns together. The brief moments of physical contact can make the movements very seductive, as they step away and return on the *ripresa* steps, and making the *volta tonda* very close to each other.

The change to *saltarelli* can connect to a sudden release into a new joyful feeling of excitement as the couple join together, then separate to circle the room, keeping eye contact all the time, and touching hands again as they pass each other.

The manuscripts do not inform us how to join hands in the *saltarelli* section. Clues may be found by looking at illustrations of couples dancing, many being featured on ornate chests given as wedding gifts, called the *cassone.* This piece of furniture was given by the bride's family and contained her personal effects. The panels were decorated with scenes relating to the theme of love, sometimes situated in a mythical Garden of Venus.

There are examples depicting couples leaping with their feet leaving the floor, appropriate for the mode of *saltarelli*. Their hands are joined with the arms raised, bringing the couple very close together, as they gaze into each other's eyes. This seemed an appropriate way of showing the joyful exhilaration in this couple dance – although floor patterns and handholds may vary to suit other imagined dramatic scenarios.

The return to formality is signalled by the *bassadanza* rhythm for the dignified ending, although the *movimenti* gestures performed in turn may still be used to demonstrate the underlying frisson continuing between the two lovers as the couple join for a final respectful reverence.

Nonsuch Dance Reconstruction (6)
Italian *Ballo* for Two Couples – *Anello*

Reconstruction: Nonsuch Dances from the Court of Europe, Volume 2, Domenico da Ferrara.

The title of this dance means 'a ring' which could refer to the way the four dancers face into the centre, forming a ringed space, which they move around. During the dance the men and women change places, giving an opportunity for exchanges between the different couples as they make their *movimenti* gestures. The dance begins with *saltarelli*, and ends with a fast *piva* section, as the original order of the couples is re-established. Actors can execute each section with a different rhythmic feeling, and consider how this might refer to a particular *misura*, and how these changes of rhythm may expose different relationships between the dancers. These choices may in turn construct the dramatic narrative.

Table 3.1: Options for the Misura *Sequences in the* Ballo Anello

Section	Choreographic description	Misura options
Following	Couples following each other, relating to partners	*Saltarelli* to travel freely around the room
Changing	Changing places, meeting partner of other couple	*Saltarelli* hopped step, but feeling of *Quadernaria* to maintain the square formation
Turning	Turning in place with a double step	*Bassadanza* for a slow turn
Returning	Circling behind partner	*Piva* for fast run to return to original place

Summary: Dynamics in Spatial Patterns and Rhythmic Changes

Themes of love and romance are certainly not overtly discussed in the dance treatises; however, the aim of the activity is clearly meant to incite admiration in the observer. We can imagine Romeo as being one of these observers who admires the grace that Juliet demonstrates in her dance. An overall movement style can be maintained while the spacing and timing of the dance communicates the drama of the scene. If the emotion is played out in a dance, the rhythms may change accordingly, and a dramatic narrative may be constructed to match the choreographic structure.

Further Research Springboard

- Text:
  - Shakespeare's *Romeo and Juliet* centres on the houses of Montague and Capulet under the rule of the Prince: research historical models used for these family hierarchies.
  - The Italian Petrarchan sonnet form used in English literature: how would a lover address the person being admired in poetry and dance?
- Image:
  - *Cassones* were painted wooden chests given as wedding gifts and often have dance depicted, such as Michele Ciampanti's *The Wedding of Antiochus and Stratonice* (cassone panel).
  - An illustration of three dancers joined together is found in Guglielmo Ebreo, *On the Practice of Dancing,* 1463.
  - Portraits of the ruling families in the dukedoms of Italy display the clothing worn for formal occasions. The dancers in the Nonsuch Dance Reconstructions wear costumes based on the paintings by Leonardo da Vinci of the court of Milan, as exhibited at the National Gallery, London.
- Music:
  - Set dance forms with one musical rhythm throughout (e.g. *bassadanza*) to which any sequence of steps can be performed in the constant rhythmic mode.
  - Fifteenth-century musical compositions particular to the dance choreographies: *balli* (Nonsuch Repertoire of Italian Dances).
  - Music that changes rhythm constantly: different time signatures, unrecognizable structures.
  - Musical improvisations on a structural theme.

4

SHAKING WITH SHAKESPEARE: COURT AND COUNTRY

I have the back-trick simply as strong as any man in Illyria!

SIR ANDREW AGUECHEEK TO SIR TOBY BELCH,
IN SHAKESPEARE'S COMEDY *TWELFTH NIGHT* OR *WHAT YOU WILL*,
ACT 1, SCENE 3,
PERFORMED AT THE MIDDLE TEMPLE, LONDON, 1602

Within the Time Frame

- Mid-sixteenth century to early seventeenth-century England.

- Shakespeare's lifetime (1564–1616).

- London hosts one of the royal courts of Europe, with ambassadors frequently visiting other courts to establish marriages to strengthen political alliances.

- Dance is used at state occasions for courtiers to meet ladies to potentially lead to marriage.

- Dances related specifically to each nation, especially France, Spain and Italy, but were also danced in the royal courts of other countries.

- Courtiers trained in dance as a personal skill required for a Renaissance man to display his physical abilities in performance, connecting to display of the body through a visibly defined musculature.

- King Henry VIII (1491–1547) used pageantry as part of Tudor court display.

- Queen Elizabeth I (1533–1603) progressed around the country to gain loyalty from those living in the countryside, who performed dances in her presence.

- King James I (1566–1625) upheld the use of the court masque as a theatrical presentation of dance and music based on coded mythical themes, followed by revels for his courtiers to join in the social dances.

- Plays included dance as scenes to develop the drama, and as a pastime after the performances at the public theatres, uniting the audience through after-show jigs.

- Players in the theatre would represent all levels of society, with particular dance forms attached to different characters.

An Actor Prepares to …

- Use images to maintain a dance style in performance, including poetic descriptions of dance and stylized interpretations of animal movement.

- Develop musculature through physical exercise, concentrating on the calf muscles of the legs.

- Become skilled in jumping in the air and turning on the spot.

- Invent virtuosic steps as part of courtly display.

- Find practical reasons for the body to perform repetitive formal moves in a court setting.

- Develop complex rhythms made by intricate steps with variable spatial patterns.

- Work closely with a partner to perform lifts and turns together.

- Alternate between different dancing characters, establishing differences between scenes at court and in the countryside.

- Learn set choreographic structures, with variable verses and choruses.

- Learn to improvise within set rhythms and measuring phrases.

- Learn techniques to use the hand gestures to communicate intention while changing partners.

What You Will

Shakespeare's play *Twelfth Night* is set in a place called Illyria; however, it is unlikely that any of the audience would have had much knowledge of this location. It is often imagined as some exotic dukedom on the Adriatic coast, perfect for a plot that begins with a shipwreck bringing new characters into an established social world. Rather than searching for an unknown Illyria, this chapter considers connections to contemporary Elizabethan society, where dance was very much part of the physical world, with specific dance forms portraying different characters.

After Sir Toby Belch introduces Sir Andrew Aguecheek to Maria, the serving maid to his cousin Lady Olivia, the two knights discuss the need to have practical skill in dancing. The scene ends with a physical display of 'back-tricks' capering off the stage. For the courtier, dance was a necessary part of the training upon which the proficiency of the individual would be judged. Sir Andrew believes he has the necessary skills – but fails to understand many of Sir Toby's puns based on technical dance terminology. For example, references to French words are used in the scene for comic effect. The 'kickshawes' are not actual types of steps – but an English pronunciation of 'quelquechose', being the French for 'anything' or 'something', and the dance Sir Toby names as the 'sink-a-pace' is probably pronounced as 'sink-a-piss' to make the vulgar joke about bending your knees to 'pass water'. Actually, the word links to the French 'cinq pas' – a dance instruction for five steps performed in the lively 'galliard' rhythm. These types of dances would have been known by the men of the Inns of Court, including Middle Temple where the play was probably performed, as there are jottings of these dances in commonplace books.

Some titles of the dances in the Inns of Court manuscripts imply French origins, and the main treatise we have for this period is a French publication entitled *Orchesographie.* Written as a dialogue between a young man wanting to learn from his older teacher, the manual gives practical advice on how to dance social dances of the day. The sole purpose for learning this 'honest art' is to impress the ladies – in particular, the young student would like to win over a mistress through his display of physical skills, in the same way that Sir Andrew hopes to woo the Lady Olivia. The scene of a courtier wooing a lady in dance inspired an Elizabethan member of Middle Temple, John Davies, to write a poem, entitled *Orchestra*, entirely about dance, and this long poem contains images that identify the different dance styles. The titles of these texts refer to the *orchesis* of the ancient Greek theatre, but there is no longer any need to consider dances of the ancient times. The texts present dances created for their own particular time, and selected for their appropriateness for the particular occasions and to suit the person who wishes to impress with their fashionable moves.

It is possible to assume that both the audience and the actors would also have known these dances, and could identify the particular groups of people who may have danced them. For comic effect, actors may play the contradiction between what the character thinks looks good and what opinion the onlookers may have when they see this character dance: the dance may be performed incorrectly and inappropriately by the character on stage.

The movement of this period will need to match the style of the clothing, particularly for the courtiers wearing the newest fashions over their stiffened 'bodies' – the historical word for the undergarment we nowadays call a corset. The layers of clothing being worn also restricted movement: with the 'farthingales, kirtles and overskirts' for the ladies and 'doublet, trunk and hose' for the men. An examination of portraits from the period immediately makes it clear that even the all-important interactive gesture of the *reverence* will need to be different in this period. The backward leg stretching, which in previous centuries connected to the silhouette of long flowing dresses, is no longer appropriate: the freedom in the legs and chest area is not possible. Dancing in these corseted bodices will demand different postures and accompanying gestures.

It is rarely practical to teach historical dances wearing the full reconstructed costume of the period, although full practice skirts for the ladies and dancing tights for the men can suggest the main difference between the male and female partners. However, don't forget that Elizabethan boy actors will play female characters, and even a female character such as Viola in *Twelfth Night* will then appear disguised in man's apparel. Actors will need to consider the clothing of both the male and the female courtier, imagining at times what it is like to have their legs on show, and also what it would feel like to have several layers of skirt hiding their feet.

Musculature Manipulation

You must consider the musculature underneath the costume, and to undertake exercises to imagine how the image of the Tudor and Jacobean court can be projected with or without the full costume. The position of each person in society would have been easily identified by the style of their clothing, and this can specifically relate to particular movement styles for each character in a play. Considering links between the clothing and the person wearing these clothes will strengthen the philosophy that the people of the time wore the costume because they had made a choice of how they wanted to present themselves. This outward form develops into an art of display, with particular ways of moving to emphasize what should be seen. Without relying on any particular historical costume, the body moving in the dance forms should be able to imagine the dynamic that would have been felt while wearing the clothing of the day.

The Peacock Dance: Growing from Cod to Calf ...

This exercise uses the courtly dance form of the *pavan* to show different ways of embodying the dance with a specific physical style related to the fashion.

The *pavan* is a type of processional dance, often performed as part of formal ceremonial occasions, in partners, acknowledging the most important presence in the room. The order of the line-up in the dance exposes a hierachy within the social structure.

There are varied spellings of this dance. The usual French form is '*pavane*' – Sir Toby Belch refers to a version as the 'passy-measures pavan' – and it may have begun life as the *padovana*, an Italian dance from Padua. By the sixteenth century a version of the dance was known throughout the European courts.

In its simplest form, this is a very easy dance as it involves only two single steps followed by a double step (ssd). According to the tradition that is well established for European courtly dance of the Renaissance, the first step will always be the left. These pair of singles may be danced towards one side and then the other, keeping the body in place, as in the *ripresa* form. The first double then moves the body forward, beginning on the left foot. The step sequence then repeats, beginning with the right foot, going to right side then left side for the sideward singles, retreating the double with small steps starting on the right. It should move forward gradually at the end of each measure, as the steps forward should travel slightly further than the steps backwards.

The dance form of the *pavan* is a development of the *basse danse*, and becomes established in England during the reign of King Henry VIII, so it is an appropriate dance to use for such display and to step into this Tudor period. The history play in Shakespeare's collected works closest to his own time is *Henry VIII, or All Is True*, representing the Tudor court. The play includes many scenes of pageantry, with processions to demonstrate formal rituals used to establish new social structures.

A word of warning must be given when selecting recordings of music with which to practise the dancing in this period. Dance terms are frequently attributed to music that links to a dance tune, based on the regular rhythm used for that dance form, but these may be varied, modified and made more artistic for the concert performance without the accompaniment of dancing. The *orchesographie* dance manual identifies clear drum beats that match each dance, and gives musical lines to reconstruct consort music. It is advisable to begin with a musical version of a *pavan* with a strong clear beat, to which the (ssd) steps can be easily attached.

The *Pavan* Walk

It may be simply considered as walking steps, while listening to the music. It uses the single and double steps in the same (ssd) repeated pattern.

Steps and Music

It may alternate between a strong opening phrase (ssd) with a second phrase as an echo (ssd) as it retreats with less energy, influencing the musical dynamics.

Progression and Poetic Image

The structure gradually moves forward, using less floor space when retreating backwards. The dance is featured in the *Orchestra* poem to represent the moon waxing and waning, and reflects the gradually encroaching tide of the ocean upon the shore.

Neutral Version: Free Flowing Procession

Begin dancing this (ssd) by moving anywhere around the room to connect the steps to the music. Join hands with partner to move anywhere around the room as a couple – using a low handhold technique to guide the direction. The leader will need to consider the best direction for each measure (ssd) and be aware that they are now two people combined as a couple, moving around the studio space as one physical unit. (If you forget this, you may end up leading your partner into walls, furniture or other people on different trajectories!)

Early Tudor Version
King Henry's Great Matter
(Henry VIII, King of England, 1509–47)

Consider the portraits of King Henry VIII. Identify elements in the style of his costume that emphasize the body shape, and transform these elements into your own body shape as you walk:

- Shoulders are broad: imagine the upper body as one enlarged unit.

- The legs are thick and strong: root each step as you place it.

- The shoes keep the feet flat on the floor: let the full foot make each step.

Full-length paintings of King Henry VIII feature the fashion accessory of the pronounced codpiece: this visual display of manliness is deemed vital to a king, dismissing rumours of impotency, suggested by the difficulty he is experiencing producing a male heir with his first wife, Katharine of Aragon. This is the basis for the drama in Shakespeare's play. Imagine King Henry dancing formally side by side with Queen Katharine, but undergoing tension in their relationship. Following Queen Katharine in the dance could be her lady-in-waiting, Anne Boleyn. Henry will find an opportunity to dance with Anne, and this meeting will lead to her becoming his next wife. The contrast between public and private can be part of the expression in the dance, when secret moments can be communicated through the contact of eyes and hands.

Once you have established your style of moving with the (ssd) pattern both on your own and as partners, you may organize your couples into a column formation, imagining that the leading couple has prime importance. This couple now processes the group around the room. Let the status of the pair be visually apparent by how you execute the basic steps and how you project your feeling of power through the way you pose with your body while making the walking steps. Two groups, dancing in column formation, could also represent different factions in society: for, example, the French court of King Francis I meeting Henry and his entourage, as occurred at the so-called Field of the Cloth of Gold and referred to in the opening scene of Shakespeare's play; or the Papal ambassadors arriving from Italy to meet the English king to hear the request for an annulment of his marriage to Katharine. The group should project a shared image, charged with the same energy and imagining that they wear the same style of clothing, being uniform, all emphasizing the same elements in the body.

Late Tudor Version
The Peacock Dance of Queen Elizabeth
(Elizabeth I, Queen of England, 1558–1603)

Following her marriage to King Henry, Anne Boleyn gave birth to Elizabeth who would eventually become the Queen of England. Shakespeare's play *Henry VIII* ends with the depiction of Elizabeth's christening, and the prediction of the new age when she will become queen. When Elizabeth is in power as the ruling monarch, the fashions are different from those of her father's time, but the *pavan* still exists as a popular dance. One painting of an Elizabethan procession shows the queen being borne high by her courtiers. Such paintings provide us with evidence of a different musculature in the men:

- The tight-fitting bodices of the men make the waists appear slim.

- The codpiece is no longer displayed, but hidden behind the trunkhose.

- The men's legs are clearly displayed to appear long, with high garters tied on the thigh, and the contracted calf muscle being pronounced.

- The men are letting their heels come off the floor, with the back foot rising, which helps to flex the leg.

Take these ideas into a manner of walking:

- To contract the calf muscle, the stepping can be made onto the ball of the foot.

- Each step can achieve this effect of the body being elevated.

- Make high steps to the side on each single step, before lowering in a controlled way when the feet join.

- As the double moves forward, stay up on the toes to make the three steps.

- Even the steps into the backward direction can be taken on the rise.

- Being on the ball of the foot requires balance and control to look good, as you lower gently back to the floor at the end of the double steps forward and back.

The queen and her ladies-in-waiting are pictured wearing the French fashion of a V-shaped bodice and the overskirts shaped by the circular farthingale underneath, which lift the skirt slightly above the floor. Although their legs are not on show, the women by the side of the men would probably need to step in the same way to make the dancing pair look harmonious together, so the skirts would glide as they move together.

How can we describe this type of walking now? The same step sequence is being made, but the style is completely different, with different parts of the body being displayed in the dance.

The name of the *pavan* dance can link to the Latin word *pavo* used for the peacock. In this species of bird, it is the male that displays all the finery, but here, it appears that the image of the peacock is attached to the female figure of Queen Elizabeth. All courtiers wear ruffs high around their necks, but it is the ladies' ruffs which span out, suggesting the image of the peacock's tail fanning in all its splendour.

So, although the queen remains in the usual position for the female in a dancing couple, following the lead of the man to her left, her clothing signifies her importance. The male courtiers are required to display their skill by balancing on their toes, as they dance wearing their russet colours of the pea-hen, with their manliness hidden away.

Strutting

The French verb *se pavaner* – to *pavane* yourself – is very appropriate to introduce now: peacock-yourself as you dance. The Italian dance treatises in existence from the sixteenth century (from dancing masters such as Fabritio Caroso and Cesare Negri) will also introduce the term *pavoneggiare*, meaning to '*pavan*' yourself and so suggest using your whole body to display your self-importance as you survey the scene making your steps. The ruff around the neck should remind you to keep the head upright, so as you step, imagine this stiff lace collar framing your neck. Imagine how it would move as you look to one side or the other. Express your power as an elevated Elizabethan courtier as you 'strut your ruff'!

Don't Cramp your Style

The *pavan* is the slowest dance, and the slower the music the more technique is needed to balance for longer as the group steps together. Dancing with your body weight on the balls of the feet at such a slow pace means that the calf muscles in your legs will have been contracted for a long time, and it is necessary to make a stretch of the leg to extend the muscle again. If you do not stretch out this muscle then it is very likely that you will experience cramp some hours later. It is likely that this would have been a risk for the men and women in the Elizabethan time as much as now. Because of this reasoning, I believe the stretching of the calf muscle should be involved in the dance technique of the period, and the first place this can be included is in the reverence.

The Elizabethan Male Reverence

The Reverence is a lowering of the body. Having stepped forward and up, as you place the leg behind you, lower the heel and continue to bend the knee of that leg. The front leg will stay ahead and straight. The stretch of the calf muscle should be felt in the leg that has stepped back. The body must maintain its forward position as the weight of the body is lowered, imagining this to be on a vertical line through the stretching muscle in the leg. The hips should remain in line, so that the posterior is not pushed out behind. The front leg remains forward and in view, and this is the leg that is being shown by the male courtier for all those around to see. Meanwhile, the calf stretch is being made on the leg placed behind.

The sensation may not be as noticeable as in other modern stretches, but it is worth exploring how the calf muscle can be actively involved in this gesture. The regular use of this stretch while making a bow will make sure that it always has a real purpose for the individual: a demonstration of the developed shape of the exercised muscles, and a health and safety device at the same time!

The Elizabethan Female Reverence

The farthingale skirt requires a different type of Reverence. The backward step would rock the skirt back and forth, and there would be no point in putting the best foot forward, since the legs would not be visible. The lady of this period will need to lower herself into the ground to maintain her body level with that of her male partner. The sixteenth-century Italian dance manuals do give specific instructions for a *riverenza*, suitable for both the man or the lady. The feet only need to make tiny steps. One foot may move forward slightly before lowering the body: it is only one small release of the leg forward and then placing this parallel to the side of the other foot, just slightly back, and then bending both knees. Again, this should allow the calf muscle to stretch as the body is lowered, and in fact this time it is possible that both legs will receive the calf stretch.

Playing with Hierarchy: Tudor Status Cards

The above instructions are an attempt to create a neutral version of a Reverence that would be appropriate to use when dressed in the fashions of the sixteenth and seventeenth centuries. Of course, a Reverence is never made as a neutral statement in a dramatic situation, as the gesture is actually used to establish a hierarchy between the various other characters.

This gesture should always be interactive, making a connection with the person to whom the Reverence is directed, and recognizing the response that is returned. The art of self-display is being emphasized in this chapter, but it is also about how people situate themselves in a particular place in the social system, where each person has to constantly negotiate their position. Power games and social negotiation can be made visible in the way the bow is physically executed. As a new character enters the scene, the status may change, and the characters may use different Reverences at different times to signify the hierarchy. Sir Andrew probably would bow differently to his fellow Sir Toby, to the servant Maria, and then to the Lady Olivia whom he hopes to impress. He may make the gesture of a Reverence when he meets his rival Cesario, but this gesture would only be a formality, as he feels no real respect.

Comedy is also possible as Cesario is really Viola in disguise, and is a male actor playing a noble lady making a male Reverence.

The gesture is technically complete when the calf muscle cannot stretch any further; however, the placement of the head and the upper body, along with the use of the eyes, can be involved in this gesture to give information on the status of the individual in relation to the other characters in the scene. The amount of time taken to bow and the amount of bending in the upper body can all communicate a different dramatic interpretation.

This can be explored by playing a game in the studio where the level of status has to be guessed by how the characters bow to one another. Status can be allocated by the distribution of playing cards, giving each player one card and asking them to use the action of a reverencing between the group to place themselves in order from high to low. It may seem appropriate that the king should be considered the top card, so that the ace is actually regarded as the lowest number one. If you have 13 or fewer players, then you may choose to use only one suit, so that there are no duplications in the sequence. You may prefer to select from the whole pack of 52 cards, however, and let fate decide whether there are many of the same status in the society. It is particularly interesting to see the necessary complex negotiation between people who have the same or very similar status cards, as they will need to work hardest to decide who is slightly superior, just a little bit inferior, or simply their equal.

Reverence Status Game Version 1: 'Know Thyself'

The first version of this game involves the actors seeing their own card but not revealing this to the others in the room. They physically project what they know to be their status. Without knowing the value of the cards held by the others, this may result in people assuming they have more importance than they really have and lead to them placing themselves higher in the line-up. Those of low numbers may not believe that anyone can be lower than them, and this becomes particularly entertaining if two people share the same low number. It is in the middle area that it is hard to be sure where people are really placed. Once it is decided to end the game and present the line-up, the actors should make any amendments by repeating interactive reverences to each other, so that they can modify their gestures to show more humility – or possibly be required to inflate themselves further to then move up the line.

Reverence Status Game Version 2: 'Do Unto Others'

The second version of this game involves the actors not seeing their own cards – maybe holding the cards on their foreheads. In this way, the rest of the group can see your card, but it remains hidden to yourself. Make sure there are no mirrors around in the studio or other reflective surfaces that might give the game away! The player now has to work out what status card they have by how people bow to them. This version of the game allows those around to give you information of where you fit into the hierarchy – you should see how others react to similar status cards around you as well as to yourself. It may be useful to put a time limit on this game, so that the group works as quickly as possible to determine what status card they believe they have. Once everyone has settled into what they assume to be their rightful place, then someone from either end can move down the line, giving an appropriate Reverence, and if there are people not in sequence, use the bow to move them up or down the line.

Physical Variations

It should be remembered that this is a game to develop subtle variations to the basic bow. You may communicate this in how other parts of the body are moved – the head, the back, the arms, the hands – but you must not let go of the stretched calf muscle which we have identified as the requirement to feel that the bow is purposeful. The time taken to make the bow can vary and give a different feeling of status. The preparation before the bow is important – as there must be an elevation before there is a lowering of the body, so this can communicate different levels of respect. Also, you should hold onto the idea that the whole group still belongs to one court wanting to look their best as a whole, so don't let your posterior stick out unduly as you emphasize a humble position! Also, avoid adding excessive pantomimic gestures, as we are still assuming that the characters hold an ideal of being noble, even if they are low in status.

Fooled You

The jester card can be included in this game, as the character playing the fool, and he is in effect able to move anywhere in the system – next to the king as much as to the lowest born.

Court Display
Nonsuch Dance Reconstruction (7)
New Almaine

Reconstruction: Nonsuch Dances from the Courts of Europe, Volume 3 and 4.

Using the Reverence During Courtly Dance

The *Almaine* (or *Almain/Alman* and other variants) is a dance form that is recorded in the Inns of Court manuscripts, assumed by its name to have German origin. It is a dance for a couple, performed socially with a number of couples who parade around the room.

The *New Almaine* includes the instruction to 'honour' as part of the choreography, so the Elizabethan Reverence can be practised as being an integral part of the dance. To emphasize the presentational quality of this opening dance, the reconstruction uses a handhold where the lady can rest her hand on the man's slightly raised arm.

The Display of the Leg

Hops are included at the end of the double steps in *Almain* dances. The raising of the leg on the hop allows the gentleman to display his calf muscle, and for the lady to allow her farthingale to lift.

Spacing as a Group: Circular Placement

The dance progresses around the room, and forms a circle with an inside and outside circle. The steps should space the dancers evenly around the room. It is the men who must locate themselves in the centre of the room, and place their ladies on the outside. This tests the skill of stopping in a particular place, making sure the couples are evenly spaced as spokes of a wheel.

Set and Turn: A Figure for Display

The *two singles and double round* (a set of single steps and a turn on the double) is abbreviated as a 'set and turn' and is used frequently as a compound unit in many historical dances. The amount the feet are lifted on the steps can be varied, and in terms of the placement of the arms, these can be held formally or moved freely. The set of singles allow a moment of self-display, while acknowledging the partner you are dancing with. The turn double enables you to consider the others dancing with you at the same time, as well as noticing others watching the dance from around the room. There is a dialogue form to the dance, for example where the men step first to the side, then the ladies make one step, before they cross together. In this reconstruction, the *set and turn* pattern also follows this structure so that each group has an opportunity to feel they are making their statement as one group to the other.

Using the *Galliard* Rhythm

When Sir Andrew declares that he delights in masques and revels, Sir Toby quizzes him on his proficiency at performing the *galliard*. This dance was the real test of the courtier's ability, for, although the *galliard* was a couple dance between a man and his lady, sections of the dance would require the man to present a solo display of dexterous steps in front of his partner and for all the court to see. Capering steps are used in the execution of fast 'alta' dances such as the *galliard*, with others, including the *jig* and the *coranto*, also mentioned by Sir Toby.

Today, our national anthem still resounds to the rhythm of the *galliard*

– 'God Save Our Grac-/- ious Queen' –

with six beats in the measure, the syncopation occuring at the end, just as the basic performance of the '*cinq pas*' comprise four steps, a jump in the air, and a cadence to bring the feet together with an identical rhythm. To impress with the *galliard* steps, a gentleman would use the gesturing legs to cut under the feet, beat in the air and swing to different positions. Sir Andrew's '*back-trick*' would have been seen as a great feat of agility if, of course, the courtier can actually do what he says he can.

Stepping the *galliard* rhythm in dance: five steps' exercise – the tourdion step

1 2 3 4	Four steps with a jump on the fourth beat
5	in the air
6 and	Cadence: landing on one foot, then placing the other foot forward on the floor (no body weight on this forward foot, which then begins the sequence)

It was reported that Queen Elizabeth practised the *galliard* every morning before breakfast. In 1589, when the queen was in her mid-50s, John Stanhope of the Privy Chamber reported, 'the Queen is so well as I assure you, six or seven *galliards* in a morning, besides music and singing, is her ordinary exercise'. Her intention was not to present this dance herself to the court; in any case, the steps of the dance would not be seen underneath the skirts. However, practising such a technique would prepare her for a dance to the same rhythm that required the lady to be turned by her partner as she was jumping in the air. This was the dance named *La Volta*, criticized as 'a wanton dance' in the *Orchesography*. This was partly because of the proximity of the male dancer who would take her in his arms and be allowed to hold her 'under the busk'. If the paintings we have of this dance show an accurate depiction of this lift, then the man is indeed lifting her with his hand placed between her legs, therefore it is easy to understand why the dance may be considered scandalous. To reconstruct this lift in practice depends on the structure of the costume for the lady. Whatever the specific handhold, the lifting turn is achievable when both partners jump around the same central axis.

Nonsuch Dance Reconstruction (8)
La Volta

Reconstruction: Nonsuch Dances from the Courts of Europe, Volume 3 and 4, from Arbeau, Orchesographie, 1588/1596.

Strict Embracements

Dancing the *la Volta* is a challenge for a couple to rehearse together in order to find a shared technique to jump and turn together. Pictorial evidence shows that this dance between the couple would be performed in full view of the court – the connection between the two dancers requires an intimate physical connection but a spectacular outward display as the man leaps from the floor with the lady turning in the air. Handholds in such dances were criticized by Puritan moralists as being lascivious, since they were seen to offer opportunities for partners to communicate immoral intentions.

The Arrival

The honour is used to invite the lady to dance. The phrase 'to honour' is used in this historical period for the bow made as a 'reverence' to a partner.

The Wooing of the Lady

The presenting of the hand allows the lady to join. The gentleman brings the lady to him to prepare for the turning in the air. The lady places her right hand on his shoulder, the other hand by her side to prevent her skirt lifting. The man has his left hand around her waist and his right hand at the front of the dress 'under the busk' to lift with the costume or, if preferred, on the hip of his partner.

The Processional Steps Travelling Together

The tordion step is performed (as above).

The Turning in the Air

The sequence for the feet is as follows:

1 2 Two steps (hop left, step right: the man turns clockwise a quarter-turn each step).
3   Join the feet together.
4   Bend knees to jump (continuing with a further quarter-turn)
5   in the air
6   and land with a cadence (having now moved around the circle by three-quarters).

The lady must jump in the air with her legs hanging straight down and not think about turning herself. The man is thinking of turning as he jumps with the right leg staying in place (maybe resting on his tip-toe), the left leg lifting to place the left knee behind the lady to help her turn. The combination of the step rotates the couple by three-quarters each time. By doing this four times, the man will return to end facing the front.

Processional Step Variations

Variations can be made with different floor patterns and handholds with the lady:
    Continue with the Tordion rhythm or variations. Separate away from your partner and return to the hold. Rotate with the handhold (palm to palm).

Taking Leave

After such a dance that brought two people together in such an energetic way, it must be decided how the final Reverence will be performed, and to consider how decorum may be re-established in the court. There is potential for dramatic scenarios to be played out. The dance manuals comment on the likelihood that the many turns will have left the partners in a dizzy state, and there is a concern from the moralists as to whether the lady will have lost her dignity by being bounded about in such a way. The reactions of those around this dance may suggest possible scenarios that could develop, as those figures in the paintings also appear to have opinions on what they are watching.

Nonsuch Dance Reconstruction (9)
Italian *Balletto – Torneo Amoroso* (A Love Tournament)

Reconstruction: Nonsuch Dances from the Courts of Europe, Volume 2, from Cesare Negri, Le Gratie d'Amore, 1602.

The translation of the title as a 'Love Tournament' points to the fact that a dramatic narrative may underlie the choreography of this couple dance. We may not know what the actual story is behind such a dance, and whether the two people dancing this couple dance have a particular back-story to their relationship before the dance begins. However, the reconstruction of the description of the steps shows that the dance is passionate, has confrontational moments and uses complex spatial dynamics to mimic how a battle can occur on the dance floor, seeming to draw upon the actions that would have occurred in a real tilt or joust between two characters on horseback. It is likely that in reality the courtly partners would need to be in compliance to dance, and the choreography may be using the idea of a tournament to represent two people actually enjoying the encounter. It may, however, offer scope for other theatrical interpretations, where the nature of the steps and the interactive patterning can be connected to narratives of disdain, exposing tensions within an amorous relationship, with feelings transforming to adapt to certain sections of the dance.

The overall style for the steps is reconstructed from the writings by the Italian dancing masters of the sixteenth century (Fabritio Caroso, c. 1526–c. 1605, and Cesare Negri, c. 1536–post-1604). The printed books of these masters include illustrations of courtiers in full costume, including the gentlemen with both cape and swords, and references to the ladies wearing raised footwear called 'chopines'. These books give very detailed explanations on precise steps, and rules for how to perform particular rhythms, including many variations for different sequences for the *gagliarda*. In addition, there are rules concerning matters of etiquette, including the importance of making sure your gloves are not too tight so that you don't have to use your teeth to pull them off before offering your hand to your lady. The rules for the stepping of the feet even go so far as measuring the space between the stepping feet as only being 'four fingers' breadth'. Following such rules will make the choreography of such a *balletto* feel very confined and restricted. This tense movement style is aptly suited to consider the Italian settings of the Jacobean tragedies filled with revenge and intrigue.

Table 4.1: Dance steps in Torneo Amoroso reconstruction

Italian	Definition	Placement of the feet on completion of the step
riverenza grave	slow bend	foot moves from front to back
passo grave	slow step (equivalent to *single*)	one foot stays ahead
seguito ordinario	an ordinary step (equivalent to *double*)	after three steps one foot ends ahead
seguito spezzato	a broken step	foot from behind joins the instep of front foot
continenze	side steps	feet together
pavoneggiarre	preening	feet on floor with body lifted
scorrendo	scurrying	moving on front of feet
passo puntato	stopped step	rising as feet come together, lowering heels together
ripresa	step to side	step to side, rise as foot comes to meet, then lower and close the feet together
doppio step	a double step	three steps with a rise, the fourth joining with the heels

Dramatic Narrative in *Torneo Amoroso*

The following questions are suggested to help understand how the structure of the dance may be given a particular narrative.

You can identify these sections in the Dance Reconstruction sample, and try out the spatial configurations with the steps for each section.

1   Bow and independent circles – what is the feeling to release your partner so soon in the dance?

2   Towards the Presence – preening – to whom are you looking as you move from side to side?

3   The lady scurries away – why does she leave you so quickly?

4   The man must move to the back of the room to meet her again – does he ask her to continue the dance?

5   Returning to the dance and lining up for the first dance together – is she agreeing to this willingly?

6   Face to face and passing shoulders – how does this feel, being so close to each other? What can you communicate when you step from side to side after this rubbing of shoulders? Do these feelings change when the sequence is repeated in the other direction?

7   The man bows and takes the hand of the lady – is she in full agreement with this?

8   The couple circle the room – is the lady moving freely around the man or is there tension between them during this move?

9   Separation using the spiky broken steps to end with their backs to each other – how does it feel to now have backs turned?

10   The man makes the first move and turns back, before the lady turns to respond – what does this abrupt stopped-step move communicate towards each other?

11   The dynamic between the two dancers intensifies as the stopped steps become little punctuated steps, resulting in the two dancers turning away from their partners – what do you choose to communicate with these types of steps and patterning on the floor?

12   The man moves to one side of the room as the lady waits and bows, and the lady repeats the same pattern, setting up the idea of the man and woman being on opposing sides – is this Reverence now a preparation to begin the battle?

13   The feet take on the triplet rhythm preparing to charge across the space, making the tournament reference clear with the idea of horses' hooves and the lances being struck as hands hit when the dancers pass each other – what does the hit communicate? Who initiates the action?

14   The confrontation continues as the two dancers get closer – is the tension building?

15   The lady lifts her hand to strike as they do sideward steps and finally she takes both hands to him – how does the man maintain his courtly decorum while he pacifies the lady and lowers her arms?

16   Further preening and bowing prepares for linking arms to dance to the *galliard* rhythm – what negotiation is occurring to allow both partners to circle together? Has the tension been resolved?

17   The final parade around the room and final bows to each other – how does the dance now resolve at this final moment, and what is the relationship between the two dancers at the end of the choreography?

Tudor Tasks

Nonsuch Dance Reconstruction (10)
Washerwomen's Branle

Reconstruction: Nonsuch Dances from the Courts of Europe, Volume 3 and 4, from Arbeau, Orchesography, 1588/1596 .

Beginning as a simple circle dance made of double steps revolving to the left and to the right, this dance then allows the dancers to mime actions during the chorus. While pretending to be washerwomen, the ladies wave their fingers at the men, as if reprimanding them. The slapping of the hands is described in the manual as resembling the sound of the clothes being beaten against the stones on the River Seine. This dance, reconstructed from the historical material, can justify miming other ideas in movement, and suggesting suitable choreographic structures that match activities performed by the servants of the Tudor court.

Country Matters

What of the people in Shakespeare's England who were not part of the court? What did they dance? Plays of this period mention country folk dancing communally, and it is assumed that these types of dances were handed down as a tradition, or created for special occasions when groups were gathered together. There are references to the morris dance (such as in Shakespeare's *Two Noble Kinsmen*), and a form of this dance was famously danced by William Kemp, one of Shakespeare's clown players, in which he was depicted with bells on his ankles and handkerchiefs in the air. Jigs were danced at the end of plays in London, in which all and sundry may have taken part, although the exact music and steps are not recorded in any detail. A publication appeared in 1651 entitled *The English Dancing Master*, and many of these so-called country dances may have had their origins in the tunes, steps and patterns of decades before. People having fun dancing have been captured in the art of the period, with people swinging each other around with their arms linked. I suggest that this is the first move to get everyone into a less-courtly feel and imagine how communal dance could sweep people off their feet at festive occasions. The *swinging of partners by the arm* is referred to as 'arming' in seventeenth-century notated dances, and is one of the regular requirements in the country dance form.

Swing your Partners

Choreographic structures from *The English Dancing Master* can be deciphered from the basic notation to create a variety of organized frameworks that introduce different ways of interacting socially on the dance floor. There are opportunities within each dance to change partners, to dance as the whole group, or to be part of separate groups made up of either the men or the women. A selection of simple dances is included here, in particular to consider how the elements in the dance can be treated differently in performance.

The Country Dance Structure

Verses

The basic structure of the early country dance has three verses danced in a set order:

1 Doubling – where the couple move forward and back with the double step.

2 Siding – where the couple move to the side of each partner and back again.

3 Arming – where the couple face each other and link with right arms and move clockwise around their own circle, then link with their left arms and dance the other way around.

Chorus

In between these verses there will be a choreographed section, which I will call a chorus. Sometimes this chorus may be the same after each verse, but in some dances it may be a new set of choreographed moves.

Aerial View

It is worth trying to learn the dance with this overall structure in mind rather than only as a linear sequence of moves. This will help the memory store the dance as a three-dimensional structured design. Similarities and differences in other formation-based choreographies can then be distinguished by which sections are maintained and which are changed. In fact, the actor always needs to consider the structure of the country dance as a whole, and know where each person fits into this structure. Think about how this dance looks from above, and how the patterns would be viewed as an architectural plan or as a garden design, moving from one formation to another. The verses are then important as places where the connection is restated with your own partner. The direction of the steps of each verse will relate to where the partners are standing in this formation, and this may also depend on the overall shape governing the dance.

Nonsuch Dance Reconstruction (11)
Country Dance for Two Couples – *Rufty Tufty*

Reconstruction: Nonsuch Dances from the Courts of Europe, Volume 3 and 4, from Playford, The English Dancing Master, 1651.

A dance for two couples produces a square set.

Style

The name 'Rufty Tufty' justifies this being performed in a boisterous manner.

Verses

These are in a square set.

1 The *doubling* involves the couples going toward and away from each other.

2 The *siding* means that the partners meet their partner on the first siding and their opposite on the second.

3 The *arming* is likewise first with the partner and then the opposite.

Chorus

- The chorus is the same after each verse.
- The set and turn can be made lively in country style.
- The square shape of the dance continues as couples dance away to the sides.
- The turn of the double allows the actors to see the next person they will join and dance with.

Nonsuch Dance Reconstruction (12)
Country Dance for Three Couples – *Shepherds' Holiday*

Reconstruction: Nonsuch Dances from the Courts of Europe, Volume 3 and 4, from Playford, The English Dancing Master, 1651.

A dance for three couples places the line facing the front, so there is a lead couple, a second couple and a third couple.

Style

With the title suggesting that this is a holiday for shepherds, we can imagine a festive rural feel for this dance, although the music for the reconstruction is played on a virginal, so a more sedate feeling is more appropriate on the sample. With quicker music the steps could be made much more wild and lively. However, this slower speed allows attention to be given by the actors to make the formations look aesthetically pleasing, considering how the lines established by dancers can be kept straight and with moving bodies arriving into the next position to match the phrases of the music. Although the notations do not detail whether any particular footing should be made to the steps, a decision may be agreed upon to give a uniform style in performance. Using the left foot to begin forward motion and right foot for backward has become a preference, continuing the rule established for court dances of this period.

Verses

The specific motif for this dance involves a right-hand turn, which is placed at the end of each move:

1. Doubling – with right hand crossed from the beginning, the steps made to the front of the room and then to the back.

2. Siding – the right-hand turn switches the lines from what is called the 'proper' side to the 'improper' side; after the second siding with partners it returns to 'proper'.

3. Arming likewise uses the right-hand turn to the change from proper to improper and back again.

Chorus

The choruses are different after each verse:

1. Couples form a line of men and women who follow each other back to their place.

2. Lines of men and women then make circles in their own group and revolve.

3. Partners change up the line.

Nonsuch Dance Reconstruction (13)
Country Dance for Three Couples – *Picking of Sticks*

Reconstruction: Nonsuch Dances from the Courts of Europe, Volume 5, from Playford, The English Dancing Master, 1651.

This dance is included to show how the basic ideas of the country dance form can be developed to form more complex patterns. The figures in the choreography are based on changing partners and weaving through lines, first as individuals, then as couples, and finally as a line of three.

1   The Doubling section has partners changing up the line one-by-one, allowing individuals to interact in turn with all the others in the line.

2   The Siding section is performed with the partner passing with a 'pendulum swing' motion that prepares them for the energized slip steps, where couples both alternate weaving into the centre of the space and then all around the set.

3   The Arming section leads into a weave which has been called a 'sheepskin hey'. First, the men as a line of three weave between the women, with the man who is last in line changing direction when he is circling the lady in the middle, and becoming the leader of the line. This pattern continues until each of the three men has taken the leader position and the line returns to its original order. The women's line then performs this 'sheepskin hey'.

Hey Nonny Nonny

The 'hey' figure is a very important element to country dancing, and particularly useful for training actors. They must keep flowing constantly while dancing particular spatial figures that rely on interacting with other bodies that are moving at the same time. The term 'hey' may historically refer to the weave made when a growing vine would need to thread between a trellis (suggested by the French word *haie* for hedge), and this image is useful to keep in mind. It appears obvious when only one line is moving through a line of people who are standing still (as in the 'sheepskin hey' in the *Picking of Sticks* reconstruction). However, you can 'hey' by meeting a line of people who are also moving, and weave by passing each person, alternating sides. You may learn this technique with the actors touching hands as they meet, passing by, before moving to the next person. To perform this successfully, the actor needs to see the next person by looking directly at their eyes. They need to resist the temptation to look for the hand that they will need to take. The hand will come automatically. While weaving, you should be aware of the patterning that the bodies are making together, thinking how this figure will look from outside, and imagining how this pattern would appear from above. Eye contact also allows the social interaction to continue as they look at a new partner. Using the word 'hey' as a spoken greeting can make this more important. Exercises that practise the eye and hand coordination between the group are useful: these could be conducted in a circle and require partners to change places by a signal from a look, before moving and giving hands to cross the space and take up a new position. Considering Maria's jokes in *Twelfth Night* about the dryness of hands, physical contact in a dance becomes a way to communicate your character, even in a momentary passing by, and a value judgement can be made immediately by the way the partner you meet offers their hand and makes a connection in the look.

Summary: Shape, Style, Status and Show of Harmony

Differences in dance styles between different social strata can be considered in many of Shakespeare's plays. For example, in *As You Like It*, the court and the country style could be justifiably given contrasting movement styles, and although in *A Midsummer Night's Dream* the setting is ancient Athens, the distinction between nobles and mechanicals can be physically realized in this Elizabethan fashion. Even in the fairy world, the opening discord and closing harmony between the two monarchs, King Oberon and Fairy Titania, relate to dance imagery, with Oberon refusing to join the 'ringlet' dances of the fairies. At the end of the play, the fairies' 'carole' may represent the idea of order with a circling formation. Shape, style and status are inter-related in this version of dramatic dance.

Further Research Springboard

- Text:
    - The poem of dancing called *Orchestra* by Elizabethan courtier Sir John Davies can be read as a catalogue of all dances known in England during this period, despite the story being set in ancient Greece. You can guess the dance from the images the poet uses and the rhythms of nature that he attaches to each different dance.
- Image:
    - See how portraits show stance and musculature: such as King Henry VIII, (c. 1545) after Hans Holbein, and the male courtiers appearing in Robert Peake's painting of the Procession of Queen Elizabeth I, to Blackfriars (c. 1600).
    - *La Volta* is central to the painting in Penshurst Place, Kent, entitled *Queen Elizabeth I dancing with Robert Dudley, Earl of Leicester*. You can play 'spot the difference' by comparing this painting with the very similar painting of the French Valois court of King Henri III (c. 1580.) Alongside the central dancing couple, these scenes show the courtiers assembled at a court occasion, and suggests ways that handholds can occur between partners when not dancing. These images are interpreted in the groupings used in the Nonsuch Dance Reconstruction of *La Volta*.
- Music:
    - Alongside set dance music, dance improvisation can be inspired by the lute fantasies of court composer John Dowland.
    - Thomas Morley provides many examples of songs interpreting dance rhythms. These sung madrigals can be staged and dance steps selected to fit the pattern in a creative way.

5

BAROQUE AROUND THE CLOCK: MINCING BY THE MINUET

The lines which a number of people together form in country or figure dancing, make a delightful play upon the eye, especially when the whole figure is to be seen at one view, as at the playhouse from the gallery; the beauty of this kind of mystic dancing, as the poets term it, depends upon moving in a composed variety of lines, chiefly serpentine, governed by the principles of intricacy, &c. the dances of barbarians are always represented without these movements, being only composed of wild skipping, jumping, and turning round, or running backward and forward, with convulsive shrugs, and distorted gestures.

WILLIAM HOGARTH,
'OF COUNTRY DANCING'
THE ANALYSIS OF BEAUTY, 1753

Within the Time Frame

- The Restoration in London begins in 1660 when King Charles II is crowned.
- The dance style begins in the mid-seventeenth century and continues to the end of the eighteenth century.
- The fashions include the heeled shoe for both the man and the woman.
- Accessories include wigs, hats and canes for the gentlemen, and fans for the ladies.

An Actor Prepares to ...

- Walk with a heeled shoe.
- Turn out the legs and train in a dance technique that will develop into classical ballet.
- Use the arms separately in opposition to the feet and adorn simple steps with flourishes.
- Consider how small changes to the placement of the feet can change the feel of the dance and give the character a particular way of walking.

- Develop a precise balance and poise while in motion.

- Make a distinction between gestures with the legs and postures with the whole body.

- Allow external shapes to govern all moves across the floor.

- Use dances to express extravagance within a controlled form.

- Train the body as a moving architecture, aware of complex structures in space.

- Explore caricature and commedia by purposely breaking choreographic rules.

Variety is the Spice of Life

This chapter is of particular relevance to the drama of the seventeenth and eighteenth centuries. The French plays of Molière from the time of King Louis XIV combined drama with dance interludes and were categorized as *comédie-ballets*. In Restoration London, the newly opened theatres presented comedies and dramas alongside musical interludes, with operatic shows and danced commedia pantomimes, frequently mentioned in the diaries of Samuel Pepys. Pepys also records the need to learn the new dances coming into fashion, and rather reluctantly hires a dancing master to teach the steps to him and his wife. The dancing master would teach a way of moving that would be accompanied by the fashion accessories of hand-held fans for the ladies, and walking-canes for the gentlemen, all fashionably dressed to meet in the newly established coffee houses, taking quick intakes of snuff, before commenting on the news and gossip of the town.

Newly Restored

No matter what political views may be held about the system of monarchy, the theatre student can celebrate the Restoration in London as the historical moment when the public theatres reopened and frivolous entertainment such as dancing was encouraged again as part of social life. To Londoners it felt like a new beginning. All the arts captured the jubilation of the new establishment, as those men who returned with King Charles II held their heads high in their newly fitted periwigs. Along with the new king came another newcomer onto the stage – the female player. For the first time, actresses could perform on the public stage. By her side flounced the outlandish fop with his excessive French fashions.

French Flowering

The new English king had been in exile in France. The fashion and style of Restoration London had a French flavour – and this new way of moving and dancing had been nursed in the royal court of the young French King Louis XIV. Danced spectacles called the *ballet de cour*, with the king and the nobility taking part as actors and dancers, had nurtured this style to maturity. While in exile, the future monarch of England was a visitor at the royal courts both in France and in the Netherlands. Paintings of court scenes of this period display all the details of French fashion, right down to the weave of the hosiery and the ribbons on the shoes. Louis XIV wore a glorious costume of shining gold to match the central role of the Sun King Apollo in the *Ballet de la Nuit*, and a painting of a ball at the Hague, by Hieronymus Janssens, depicts the future English King Charles dancing with his sister at the end of his exile, and displaying the same physical posing as the French king.

These continental techniques immediately took root in England. In time, it could be argued, this aesthetic would grow so plentiful that it became too florid, too rich with its swirling stems, blossoming buds and garish colours. Some actors may have a natural desire to be theatrical – so with this style you may need to be careful of going too far. Once the extremes have been found, you will need to consider how to curb this enthusiasm with a grounded technique of reality. This same decade would witness the Great Plague, followed by the Great Fire, devastating the daily lives of all Londoners.

Baroque style continued to prosper well into the eighteenth century, and dancing manuals established codified movement techniques and technical illustrations. The painter and engraver William Hogarth caricatured the poses of different city characters in prints such as *The Rakes Progress*. The figure of the dancing master is clearly identified by his extravagant pose, as he instructs the rakish nobleman. Now that he has come into his fortune, this young man is willingly paying handsomely to receive instruction on how to move. The baroque dancing technique will require dedicated practice however, and the precise steps and decorative gestures may not be suited to everyone in this society: not everyone will have the propensity for such posing!

Toe the Line

So, as an actor, standing ready to enter a new age of excess, where must we start? This style begins with the feet. For now the heeled shoe is *de rigeur*, as they say in French. To make the first step, I recommend that you get yourself a pair of heeled shoes. Ladies will have their character shoes, and to them the heels are nothing new, although the sensation of their partners standing next to them with this extra height may be surprising! The male character shoe with a heel may be purchased from dance shops as a Cuban heeled shoe, used currently for Latin American dancing. Even the local charity shops may have some men's shoes styled when heels made a former fashion statement. Shoes that are now well heeled will need to be envisioned as being reheeled – literally restored – but whatever the look of the shoe, it is the sensation of the feet that must be encased with a feeling of newness, stepping into a new age with excitement.

Show a Leg

As you put on the shoes, the men feel compelled to lift their baggy sportswear to reveal their legs: 'to make a leg' is the phrase that was used for this parading of the calf muscle as a fashion statement. It begins with the heel, but it moves up the leg very quickly. Even the girls will want to lift their skirts to reveal the heel underneath. Everyone in the room should be made to feel the power of making a statement with the presentation of the foot. So step out with your best foot forward.

Stepping Out

So out we go, stepping with the heels, thinking of new height, noticing how the body is now feeling taller, and making that vertical stretch even more pronounced as you can see the world from this raised position. This is a shared sensation – as all are sharing the same elevation with all the others around you: we have all been restored, and all been given a lift as a newly ordered society, with noblemen and women chosen to be rulers in the space and preparing to have fun. Listening to a splendid triumphant-sounding overture of a baroque composer, such as Henry Purcell or George Frederic Handel, should encourage you to attach to the strong beats of each musical bar as all the instruments majestically resound together, and the body feels enlarged by the full sound of the orchestra. But this is also a period of refinement – and now this explosive energy must be contained. Although the heel is now part of the walk, it must not be intrusive to the music. Your first task is to refine the style by silencing the footfall made by the heeled shoes. Remember the motto, 'The heel must be seen – but not heard!'

Bring Yourself to Heel

What must you do to mute the sound of the heel? The first response may be to slow down and be more aware of how you place your foot while stepping. There will be no sound of the heel if the steps are gently placed. However, it will be necessary to move to the quicker rhythms of the music, so a specific technique for the whole body will need to be found.

Stay on the Ball

Speeding up the walk, thinking of the heels but not allowing any sound to be made, pushes you onto the front of your feet, even onto the balls of your feet, and, with the heels being lifted, even almost onto the tip of your toes. As usually happens with walking exercises, the actors begin to move as a pack. With everyone falling into the easiest spatial path of the track around the room, it can look as if the actors are in some form of race, panicking to get out of this trapped sensation. The stepping may be something very much like mincing – small steps, made rapidly – with the knees becoming braced, as the driving energy is prevented from going into the floor by the fear that this will create the heel drop sounds that must be avoided at all costs. No – this mincing does not signify the baroque elegance we are trying to achieve.

Sink Into it

The technique to employ must be the opposite of what we first thought. The heel must actually have full contact with the floor, but instead of hitting the surface and making a harsh percussive sound, the body must sink and soften into the movement. If the knees are bent and the weight of the body dropped through the heels then steps can indeed be done quickly and with strength of the body, but with no sound being made. With this bending action it is also possible to propel the whole body, as a vertical being, forward into space, and onto the front of the feet for a number of elevated steps before needing to sink back down once again, to recharge the walk.

The baroque dance technique, more so than other historical styles so far considered, will require the performance of steps which comprise tiny details, requiring the division of parts of the feet being used in a particular step, with different rhythmical units and specific spatial placements on the floor at the start and end of each step. It is very possible that this amount of detail will stop the actor from making a single move, as the mass of information seems to swamp the moment before it begins. So always remember: whatever the detail of the individual step, it must be a moving of the whole body somewhere in space. The floor pattern will be important to guide us. While doing this lowering and rising as part of the action of the foot, think predominantly of where you are actually taking your body in space. Don't lose that basic need: the body must want to move somewhere with determination.

Historical Dance Term: *Mouvement*

So the lowering of the body through the heel, while also removing the unwanted sound, prepares the body for the lift and the rising step. This is the *mouvement* of the noble dance. The dancing masters upheld the need for all dance to be made graceful by employing the movement of a combined sink and rise to begin the steps, and visual artists often depict this moment when trying to capture the moment of dance in action.

Turn Out Well

Appropriately for this period, it is the French, in a saucy quip, who have taught us to 'open our legs'. No longer do we need to keep the toes on parallel straight lines, as we were required to do to please the Italian dancing masters of previous centuries. Now the leg starts to turn the foot out, away from the body. Eventually it will lead to the turn out of the leg used for the classical ballet technique, but for the moment it should not be excessive and should feel as a natural opening of the leg rather than anything tortuous. We may need to travel rapidly with the body sinking and rising, not only forwards and backwards, but also crabwise, from side to side; the turning out of the leg makes this easier, with the toes pointing away from the heel. As the body is taken in a new direction, the foot slides along the pathway, the heel connects with the vertical axis of the body, and the toes point away from this line, at probably no more than a 45-degree angle.

Mirror on the Wall

This turned-out positioning also means that the person doing the moves can make the onlooker see the heel even more, and check that this is being decorously displayed by noticing the reflection in the mirror on the wall of the dance studio. Here, a glance into the Hall of Mirrors in Louis XIV's Palace in Versailles offers an indication of how self-image is constructed during this historical period. In such a room, where the dance can be seen by the assembled court, the moving body is reflected back to the performer. The technique of this baroque dance, called *la belle danse* or noble dance, is perfected by having a dancing master offering specialized instruction of this codified technique, but the nobility must consider their own reflection to check the position of arms and legs, conforming to the ideal visual aesthetic. As a courtier in Louis XIV's royal court, many hours would be spent practising new dances in preparation for official occasions. The self-image is something that is seen from head to toe – or rather, inversely, from heel to hat – and the legs and arms are part of the ornamentation giving decoration to the moving body, as branches emanating from a central noble trunk. In the French royal court, King Louis XIV would dance as a principal figure in theatrical display, for example performing the role of the Sun King Apollo in the *Ballet de la Nuit*. This idea of having your own power reflected in all those around you is a useful way to boost your ego and raise your self-esteem.

Taking Note

This self-image is something that must be constructed from the feelings of the movement. It is worth looking at samples of the dance notation established as part of Louis XIV's Academie de la Danse – arguably the first institution established to codify a particular dance style for a nation. From this French academic position, the word choreography is used literally to mean writing the dance in symbols, combining the melody of the music, the track made on the floor by the dancers and the steps matching the space on the floor with the time in the music. Published first in France in 1700, dances were recorded as notated scores with the tune of the music, the system then used by dancing masters in England and continuing throughout the eighteenth century. Although to learn the notation fully would require a fair amount of time and concentration, in order to become conversant with all the details, a brief look at the basics can help us understand what underpins the system as a whole. We can at least identify the types of things that were considered important by the practitioners of these dances. The notation analyses the action of the feet in detail, and this analytical approach will now add to what we as actors have been exploring in an expressive way.

Ticking off

The step starts with a mark that appears as a large full stop – making a clear point on the page – the beginning of the step. We can imagine that this is where the heel is placed, since we have so far placed much emphasis on how this has rooted our position in space. The line stemming from this point will tell us the type of things to do to make this a particular type of step, with moments of bending, rising, lifting, hopping, leaving the ground or turning in space. At the end of each step there is a tick away from the line to indicate which way the foot is facing. To explore this in simple terms, we can call it a 'toe-tick'. With that basic amount of information it is now possible to move around the room and end step patterns with a pose, thinking about where the foot is placed in relation to the fixed heel and pointing toe. You will notice how much more precise it is to place the feet when thinking about the relationship between heel and toe on the ground. This unit is the foundation: the secure placing of the feet underneath the body. It is good to consider this as an underlying structure for the movement, as the body above is making a posture: the whole body settles in line with the feet, balancing between the two legs placed on the floor.

Now it is worth combining some of the positions which will have appeared during the expressive dance exercises of posing in new positions, and to think about how the exact placements of the feet that were made during these exercises can be analysed and recorded. The feet positions can be organized in relation to what we can call the '**axis-line**'. This is a vertical line that can be imagined as cutting the body through its centre. Five positions are identified as the most symmetrically balanced with this axis-line, and they are used frequently in constructing choreographies comprising precise use of steps in spatial patterns.

The **first position** requires the placing of the heels together, directly on this axis line, but with toes pointing away. The **second position** has the legs open, but with the feet still placed under the hip, evenly distanced from the axis-line. The **third position**, has one heel in the instep of the foot, both lined up on the axis line. Putting one of these feet forward and opening the legs on the axis-line will produce a **fourth position**. The **fifth position** brings the feet together again, one heel touching the toe of the other foot, but with the toes still angled away and the axis line still cutting the body evenly. These were called the *bonnes positions* in the first published notation of 1700, which we could translate as the 'good' positions. Following these five positions are another five: *des fausses positions*. These are not 'bad' in the sense that they should be avoided, but considered 'false' positions which convey a different non-noble character because of the direction in which the toes are pointing. They were used in Restoration theatre to create commedia and pantomimic characters.

On the Dot

A little dot placed at the end of the toe-tick in the published notation signifies that only the toe is touching the ground. As you move around making your postures and placing your feet, now let one of your feet rest only on the toe. This is a gesture of the foot, with no weight of the body resting on that foot. Now combine making positions, sometimes with the full foot placed and sometimes with the toe just touching the ground. Training your awareness of the difference between when you allow a foot to take the weight of the body and when it is simply placed on the floor is vital for this precise style of movement. This is the basic distinction between making a gesture or a posture: placing your body weight fully into the stance or leaving it resting on the floor.

Equilibrium

While moving with a rise and fall gracefully through the space, and arriving at different positions of the feet, there must be a momentary suspension of the body. This is technically called finding the *equilibrium*: balancing in space while maintaining the vertical axis of the lifted body, with the horizontal turn out of the legs. Practise stepping onto the toe of one foot, and bring the other foot from behind, but before placing it forwards have a moment where there is a suspended balance. The heel of this back leg will momentarily settle at the heel of the supporting leg as it passes through to take the next step. As this is a balancing step, it is a test to see how long the body can hold that moment of suspension. One way to practise this is to go from side to side, finding this state of equilibrium while you balance on the toe of one foot – moving the body from side to side, stepping to one side onto the toe, then bringing the other foot behind to rest on the heel. Now repeat this with the *mouvement* of the sink before the rise: sink on the supporting foot as the free heel is balancing, then take the step onto the foot and repeat this action.

Once you have mastered this *balance*, alternating both to the right and left, it is necessary to achieve this action while making travelling steps. A single step in this baroque technique is called a *demi-coupé*, with only one transference of weight made onto one leg. The equivalent of the previously used 'double step' is given the name *pas de bourrée*, where there are three steps linked together. A *pas de bourrée* is also called a *fleuret*, meaning a flower: we can think of the three steps linked as one sequence as petals connected together. The *mouvement* is placed at the start of each sequence, with the state of equilibrium in the body as the steps are made.

The Triple Rhythm *Fleuret* Exercise

I have found that using a piece of music with a strong pulse of three in a bar is the best way to begin exploring stepping with the rise and fall, and achieving the flow needed for the execution of a *fleuret* triplet step in baroque style. Begin walking on each of the three beats in the bar. To connect to the musical structure, emphasize the first beat, first with the heel and then with the sinking of the body. The sinking move should become the preparation for the lift of the body. The first beat in the music should be accented by the body rising as you step forward, momentarily finding that equilibrium on the first step, but continuing to dance forward for the following three steps. Only at the very end of the third step should the body lower to prepare for the next *fleuret* step forward.

Serpentine Flowing

It is very likely that doing the previous walking and posing exercises with such precision and thinking about the placement of limbs and timing with the music will have made the room appear as if it were full of mannequins, all moving in mechanical ways. The use of notation and fixation on the sculpturing of positions contributes to this rigidity. However, according to aesthetic criticism of the time, straight lines and angles are to be avoided as much as possible. So now, we need to consider the flow of the movement to make this skeleton of the historical style come alive with the swirling movement patterns of the baroque sentiment contained in the music, the architecture and the visual arts.

As an artist, William Hogarth put forward a theory of an ideal aesthetic in his *Analysis of Beauty*. Awareness of movement patterns is a very important part of this cultivating process. In particular, Hogarth emphasized the curves organically occurring in nature, and from this analysis, he identified the 'S' swirling shape as the way to add graceful flow to all patterns. Exploring this with the arms and hands is easy: move the limbs in a flowing way that makes endless curves in the space. Add this to the walking steps and see how your steps can also make flowing patterns around the room, including moments of gesturing and posing when the arms and legs come to a momentary pause, and then continue on your curvaceous way.

Arm Ornamentation

Freely exploring the serpentine flowing patterns with the arms is an expressive way of exploring the ornamentation that needs to occur in this style of movement, in dancing and even in walking with style and moving from one position to another. However, rather like the exercises to explore the walking with the heel, the specific use of the arm motion needs to be refined to have intricacy and delicacy. While the expansive use of the arms will maintain a flow and an energy that will drive the body and make the actor feel confident, it is also likely to result in a lot of flailing around, with pointless gesticulating showing a lack of control. While this wafting and waving can be immense fun, it needs to be governed by a precise shaping of the space.

Using the concepts of balance and equilibrium, we can begin to develop the control and precision needed for the arm ornamentation. Visualize the vertical line cutting the body in two and don't allow the swinging arms to cross to the other side. The arm will now only be gesturing in the space on one side of the body. Now that the arm is restricted to making curves in one half of the body-space, it is possible to find more detailed articulation using different parts of the arm. In fact, the arm is no longer to be considered as one whole unit, but divided into upper arm, elbow, lower arm, wrist and hand. Explore the articulation of the different parts of the arm. Circle the hands from the wrists: outwards and inwards, one hand then the other, both together. While keeping that fluid movement of the wrists, bring both hands closer to the imagined vertical line and find the curve that encloses the shape. You should be able to see the wrists in your peripheral vision as you make the curving shapes. From this curving position, hold your elbows in place. They should feel lifted from underneath, so that the front arm can now gesture in a circular way, towards the vertical line but not crossing over this, and outwards away from the line without pulling the elbow away from its suspended position in space. You can explore this rule by using a partner to stand behind and be a support for the arms, placing their hands underneath the elbows, and checking that the arcs are made in the precise area of body-space. Even when the lower arms are dropped down, the precise placement of the elbow and the flowing flexibility of the wrists need to be maintained.

Baroque Gesture and Arms Opposition

Let us return to the activity of moving around the room being fully aware of where you are placing your feet. Now it is time to add the movement of the arms with the feet. The basic aesthetic applied in this period is that the arms should be placed in opposition to the position of the legs. The arms offer a counter-balance to the shape being made with the stepping legs.

While this might appear a complicated idea, simply step forward with one leg and let the opposite arm swing forward. Set off on a walk and let the swinging arms match the steps in opposition. This of course is the natural opposition swing of the arms when going for a stroll, and if we were simply walking down the street we would never question this idea. Now, however, with the dance style in question, this arm has to be imbued with the power of a gesture of greeting to communicate with your dancing partners and your audience.

Try to continue this same counter-opposition swing as you step, now with the arms being lifted further. Raise the elbows so the hands can make a flowing gesture to those others you see in the space. Make sure that the gesture is placed on the opposite side to which you are stepping. Instead of stepping, now hop and gesture with the free leg. As this leg lifts towards the person you have in your line of vision, lift your opposing arm to give the circling wave to this particular person.

In other words, when a leg is placed or lifted forwards on the right side of the body it should be balanced with the left arm being forward. Again, when a leg is placed or lifted forwards on the left side of the body, it should be balanced with the right arm being forward.

Try this now with steps going backwards. For now every step backwards will leave the other leg as the front leg, and it is this front leg that must be opposed by the arms. So as you step back with the right leg, it is the right arm that now goes forward to make the gesture. Similarly, as you step back on the left, the revealed right side needs to be opposed with the left arm gesture. When the right leg is placed backwards on the right side of the body, then the left side is in effect forward in space, so the right arm must oppose the position.

Repeat the exercise of walking and making statuesque postures. Position the arms so that they give an opposition to your stance, as an ornament to your posing.

Honouring your Partner and Showing Courtesies

Considering how much emphasis has been placed on gesturing and posing towards each other, it may seem that extra moments for making a Reverence in this style would be extraneous. Far from it! There is a need to use the bow and curtsy at every opportunity, and for this reason it is important to consider the essential elements needed, so that it does not simply become an embellishment that is thrown away carelessly, but something that puts more meaning into the moment.

From the basic analysis of the historical manuals, the moves of the honours are described simply and are easy to execute, but having mastered these instructions it will be necessary to consider how variation in performance can be included to allow more complexity in the communication. Remind yourselves constantly of what the phrase 'to reverence' actually means – an action of looking at someone and then allowing this gesture to continue further communication: 'to look and to look again'. How the body is placed at this moment of Reverence and what happens with the body during the action of re-looking will be an important way to make this perfunctory activity part of an interactive dynamic, where individuals can communicate intentions which, if required, may then be discerned by the onlookers. The actor should comply with the general historical instruction, but find a way to give it a specific interpretation.

The Historical Dance Analysis: Using the Placement of the Limbs

Standard ways of making an honour are included in the dance manuals of this period, with sketches illustrating the shape of the body at the moment of bowing. This is a good place to start, but it will be necessary for the actor to consider how to play physically with these rigid examples in a dynamic interactive way.

First Position Curtsy

The lady makes her curtsy by using the first position with the feet. This allows the axis-line to be emphasized as the lady lines up in front of whomever she wishes to acknowledge. With the feet in this position it feels like a closure, a full-stop punctuating the walk. The fluidity is found again by the sinking into the floor: the heels are lowered and the knees bend to lower the body further. The legs of course are not seen underneath the skirt; indeed the fashion may extend the skirts further with hooped petticoats called *panniers* extending to the sides. Even so, this exact placing of the feet should give the feeling of symmetry and balanced proportion, and the idea of a *plié in first position* becomes a vital part of the technique for using the bend with the knees over the feet to the side to strengthen the legs for elevation, in preparation for leaving the floor with a jump. From this sinking in the curtsy, the body is ready to rise into the next step made by the body, be it a simple walking step or the beginning of a dance move.

Honour Stepping Forward

The gentleman of this period will 'make a leg' by stopping when his leg is forward, placed in a fourth position. He maintains this placement with each leg on either side of the axis-line, and by bending he will lower into the floor. It is the back leg that will bend to make this move, to allow the front leg to remain presented forward. While sharing similarities with the so-called Elizabethan bow, differences of style and sentiment will be added that are peculiar to this period.

Honour Stepping Backward

One different Reverence from this period occurs when a gentleman steps back away from the presence he is honouring. To step back to make a Reverence, a leg must gesture to the side. As the gentleman steps back, then, the other foot is placed to the side at second position, resting on the toe as a gesture. (It would be appropriate to place a dot on the notation for this foot, to signify the resting foot on the floor.) So if the right leg steps back then it is the left that is placed resting on the toe. Now the bending is not with the legs, which remain in this balanced position, but with the upper body making the curve. So the feeling is a lift of the upper carriage, as if you needed to peer over a wall. The spine stretches as the neck lifts and the head moves up and forward, to make the shape of the bow.

The Laban Dance Analysis: Using the Architecture of the Space

The idea of peering over a wall is a good image to have in mind when instructing an actor to make a Reverence stepping back. The whole body is involved in creating this feeling. Where are the feet placed to prepare for this move? How does the head move to do this looking action? What limbs are working together sequentially to make this move? What is the overall shape of the action? How does the move of the bow resolve as you return to your stance, stepping away from the imagined wall?

Placing the physical activity within an imagined spatial construct gives a holistic intention to the movement: no longer are you simply making a shape, but using this shape to interact with the space around you. Holding this body shape image in mind may prevent the bow becoming a florid empty embellishment: this type of extravagant bow fails to connect with the thing being honoured, and instead becomes simply a show-off display of the individual. Of course it is very easy to do this flouncy type of display in the costume of the Restoration period, with the lace décolletage on the sleeves, the feathers of the hats, and the ribbons on the shoes all adding a frilly frothiness to the look. The picture of the period would not be complete without these elements. However, these eccentric accessories will need to be attached to a central core. Similarly, gestures with fans and posturing with canes will need to feel part of the body communicating as a unified whole. Specific use of these props can create character and show different social interaction, but the individual needs to connect these mannerisms to a dynamic system that has its own logic. One way this logic can be discovered is by developing the idea of the body as an architectural structure, and the actor can use this understanding to create a tool to assist dynamic interaction with other players.

The use of the architecture of the space is a fundamental part of the Laban approach. The three dimensions are used to create flat *architectural planes*, imagined to be cutting the body space into three: the *vertical*, *horizontal* and *sagittal* planes. They artificially divide the space into three, and one cannot in reality exist without the other two, but the body can actively make use of these constructs by emphasizing a different plane for a different way of interacting during the bow. These can be given the simplified names of *Door*, *Table* and *Wheel*. They can be used by the actor when making a Reverence to emphasize a different reason for the bow, and connecting the feeling with a particular shaping of the body, as a way of refining the gesture and making it very specific to the situation where it occurs.

The Door of Adoration

A Reverence is a moment of meeting.

You have arrived at a point of social interaction where you must acknowledge where you stand and the space ahead of you, where others are positioned. So, to use this architectural approach, imagine you are standing in the frame of a door as you meet someone and prepare to bow: how is your stance in that frame able to show your feelings at this moment of meeting? What feelings can be attached to different places in this door? Are you lifted and in awe of the person ahead of you as you stand, aware of the high part of the door? Are you sinking despondently and neglected as you hang at the lowest place of the door? Imagine a sequence of different sensations for the moment of meeting, and situate them somewhere in this flat door plane, from low to high. While walking around the room, stop when you interact with a fellow actor and strike a pose in the imagined door frame: you may wish to use your arms to emphasize this shape, but the arms must stay within the door frame, so moving up and down is allowed without moving the arms forwards into the space. For this exercise you must try to keep as flat as possible, trying to communicate your sensation by the shape of the body in this frame. You can lift the body by rising through the feet onto your toes, or sinking as low as possible by bending the knees, but try to keep the spine connected to the vertical axis as much as possible.

How you place yourself on the vertical plane can establish meaning in the stance of your character.

The Table of Benediction

A Reverence is a moment of interaction.

Your body shape connects to the other person with whom you are interacting. The horizontal plane cuts through the middle of the body. It is again a flat plane that surrounds you. Imagine you are standing in the centre of this flat plane: it is almost like standing in the middle of a table. As you must be able to see the person you are honouring, they are placed in front of you, but your interaction can be imagined as occurring anywhere on the edge of this table plane. If you use your arms to communicate your moment of connection, then the limbs can move anywhere around this horizontal area, but should not move up or down. Try out movement on this plane and then consider the person standing in front of you, where you are directing the gesture. You may wish to welcome the person by reaching forward. You may intensely connect with the person in front of you as one special person, almost reaching out to bless the person who you connect with, imagining your connection is being channelled directly forward from your central point to meet theirs. You may try to stay neutral, with your interaction being balanced on either side, not reaching out at all. You may even be making a reverence outwardly but not wanting to really connect in any way, and this sensation of pulling away may be located in the backwards part of the horizontal plane area.

How you engage your surrounding space can determine your character's level of social interaction with other characters.

The Wheel of Submission

A Reverence establishes the status of the situation.

The act of bowing is to make a curving shape with the body. Moving through the sagittal plane can be imagined as a wheel that moves forward, down, backwards and upwards. During a Reverence the lean of the body may come to rest at any point on this circular pathway, and the feeling of importance and humility may be sensed differently. This movement may be made in a small way by the use of the head with the shoulder area. The result may begin with a feeling of pride (typically when the head is held aloof in an upper backward position), moving through different levels of bowing, from giving honour but maintaining your feeling of self-respect (with the head tilting forward but remaining high), to giving in completely to the power of the person you are bowing to (dropping the head more forward and further downward), or even displaying fear or retreat (as when the head is dropped but the shoulders are pulling back and downward). The smallest change on this 'wheel of submission' should give you a different feeling in the type of Reverence you are making.

The curve your body makes can be used to express how your character is responding to the dynamic relationship in a reverence.

Now it is time to place all these elements of stepping into what has been regarded as the main dance of presentation in this period: *The Ballroom Minuet*.

Minuet Step

The minuet rhythm is a triple rhythm, but should be counted as a dance with six beats. The basic minuet step combines one *demi-coupé* followed by a *fleuret*. In simple terms, this is the same in essence as one single step followed by a double step. It is possible to learn this rhythm by simply stepping out the pattern as in a circle dance, for example the *branle* dances of earlier periods. In fact the step pattern resembles the earlier dance of a *branle-simple*, which during the six beats of the measure would take the form of a double step (starting left) and then one single step (to the right). During the moments for a pause, the feet would join together but there would not be any change of body weight. In summary, the elements are:

- Six beats to the bar.
- *Branle-simple* pattern.
- On counts 1, 2, 3: double step to the left (stepping on the left foot, right foot, left foot).
- On count 4: pause as the right foot joins but without taking any body weight.
- On count 5: single step to the right.
- On count 6: pause as the left foot joins but without taking any body weight.

To connect this to the Minuet music, the first beat begins with the step to the right (as count 5 in the *branle-simple* pattern). In *The Ballroom Minuet*, the first step of every minuet measure begins on the right step. The right leg begins every minuet step, so once you have mastered the step, you should be able to continue confidently knowing that it is always the right foot that begins each measure. This will allow you to focus on other matters, such as how to look your best while performing this dance as your opening dance at the court, as indeed it becomes the fashion: the *danse à deux* where two people are on show. I recommend that everyone takes time to really learn the step together, and using this circle exercise will allow you to gradually add more style to the body as the swaying circle dance is matched to the minuet music.

Start by stepping to the right side on the first beat; then follow this with three steps travelling to the left, beginning on the left foot, then right, then left. In this formation, the single step travels to the right, the double step moves towards the left of the circle, and as you make the double you must decide which leg goes behind or in front as you travel crabwise. The basic minuet pattern performed as a circle dance is:

- On count 1: single step to the right.
- On count 2: pause.
- On counts 3, 4, 5: double step to the left, crossing feet behind and in front as required.
- On count 6: pause.

This circle dance as a whole will still travel slightly to the left.

Of course, this is not the minuet dance as such, but only an exercise to make sure that you physically understand the rhythm of the steps and to make the pause moments very clear. In this circle dance, the pause is also preparing for the change of direction to be made by the foot that has just joined, but without making any change of body weight.

Still keeping the same pattern as the *branle-simple*, we can add the qualities that we have been exploring in this chapter as a baroque style: the turn out, the bend and rise, and the balancing.

- First add the turn out of the legs.
- On the pause moment, the supporting leg will be joined by the heel of the other foot, which will be suspended in the air in the state of *equilibrium*.

- Now add the bending and rising before each step unit.

- The *mouvement* will occur after the moments of equilibrium during the pause between the two units (on counts 2 and 6), allowing the rise to occur on the steps made on count 1 and count 3.

The single step is now starting to resemble the *demi-coupé* and the double step is becoming a *fleuret* step as you rise onto the first step and remain lifted as you make the two further steps, before bending on the pause, ready to make the next *demi-coupé* of the next minuet measure. Dance this continuously to find the flowing sequence that fits rhythmically to the minuet music.

Now we must alter the directions – for the minuet step as one unit must move with the *demi-coupé* and the *fleuret* combined, and the whole measure must take the body into one of the travelling directions:

- Minuet forward.

- Minuet backward.

- Minuet sideward to left.

- Minuet sideward to right.

Some have suggested that the word 'minuet' has something to do with the small size of the steps taken. Even if this cannot be confirmed, it is a very useful thing to say at this stage. The steps for this type of dance do not need to be enormous. Each measure will take the body in a particular direction – it may require a number of these steps to travel any significant distance. When making steps in the sideward direction, a decision must be made which feet will cross behind, so that the steps flow easily as one combined measure. To alternate smoothly between the different directions will take practice, although the fact that the basic step always begins on the right foot should soon make you feel secure with each first step in a new direction. Although dancing masters sometimes developed variations by altering the rhythm with hops, this basic step in the four directions can easily be combined to make choreographies to minuet music of varying speeds.

Nonsuch Dance Reconstruction (14)
The Ballroom Minuet

Reconstruction: Nonsuch Dances from the Courts of Europe, Volume VI, The Ballroom Minuet, based on Rameau, Le Maître à Danser, 1725.

Established as the dance for a couple at the beginning of any formal ball, this set pattern of figures was established and recorded by the dancing masters in both France and England. Consider how each section has a different display quality, becoming aware of how the shape in space allows moments to make contact with partners and the onlookers.

Table 5.1: Spatial patterns in The Ballroom Minuet

Section	Spatial pattern	Minuet step pattern
Opening honours	Steps with honours to acknowledge the onlookers at the front and sides, and ending facing the partner.	Establishing equilibrium in preparation for beginning the minuet step.
Arrival	Connecting as a couple, moving forward, turning with partner to then move into diagonal positions of the performing space, with the lady facing forward, and the man having his back to the 'presence'. The 'presence' is the word used for the spectators in a formal setting.	Minuet steps travelling one backward and two forward. Man makes sideward step as lady moves around him, then they pivot together. Two sideward steps always keeping your front towards partner.
The Z figure (*developed from the S curving 'serpentine' shape*)	The Z shape is made on the floor, by first going to one side, then crossing the space, then making the final line of the Z. Always face your partner when making a turn of the body. It is helpful to think of crossing a bridge over an imagined river: you must return on the same pathway, crossing the same bridge.	To make a Z figure: 2 left sideward; 2 forward to cross; 2 right sideward. Repeat same steps to return on the same Z track.
Giving hands: right hand turn left hand turn	Partners meet with right hands making a turn to end in the side of the space diagonally opposite. Repeat with the left hand to return back to place.	To cross sides: 6 forward. Repeat to return.
Final figure: two-hand turn	Spiralling towards centre to join together. The man offers hands with palms downward. The lady places her two hands on his. The man moves backwards, leading the lady in a circle around the room to end in the centre, towards the back to the space.	Approach: 2 forward. Joined: 5 forward for lady and backward for man as joined. Retreating: 1 backward to open and face front.

Baroque Dance Choreographies

Having mastered making set patterns using the same basic step, it is useful for actors to consider how playful they can be in a dance, adding ornamentation with hops and poses to these basic units of *demi-coupé* and *fleuret* that were mastered in the minuet. Use arm ornamentation, and connect more with partners with these gestures to make your dance more florid. Making serpentine shapes that resemble the historical notations will give a real feel for the expressive style of moving that the people of this period were trying to achieve. While moving to music, an imagined dialogue should develop in the dance between partners that matches the musical phrasing, considering where a step ends and another begins, or how an actor might complete a sequence and then allow another actor to continue the dance, as in a spoken conversation. The mirror symmetry may also mean that partners now use opposite feet to dance the same steps. The next dance reconstruction is constructed as such a choreography, showing how simple steps can be repeated in a different order and to make different baroque-style symmetrical patterns.

Nonsuch Dance Reconstruction (15)
Bourrée

Reconstruction: Nonsuch Dances from the Courts of Europe, Volume VI, The Handel Bourrée, sample choreography by Peggy Dixon.

Bourrée Variations with the *Demi-Coupé* Step

Posing: *balance*

- Use single steps either to the side or forwards and backwards to make a connection to your partner and to show reverence at moments in the dance.
- Place the feet in one fixed position, with arms held in opposition, to punctuate the phrasing.

Bourrée Variations with the *Fleuret* Step

Run and hop: *fleuret* and *contretemps*

- Use the arm gestures to oppose the leading foot of the *fleuret.*
- Flick the wrists for the hopping on the first step to perform a *contretemps*.
- Use the sequence to move in mirror symmetry with partners side by side.
- Use the sequence to make circles on your own side of the floor.
- Extend the number of steps to make patterns around the space.
- Alternate the sequence of steps to create different phrases, such as beginning with the hop first.

Run and jump: *fleuret* and *jeté*

- Add a small jump forward at the end of the triplet step.
- Use the sequence to move around the room, with the jump taking you more forward.
- Use the sequence to move around your partner, and synchronize the moments when you jump together.

Historical Reconstructions as Show Dance

Specific baroque dance moves are altered to match particular musical forms. As well as dances for couples, these include some dances for specific numbers of dancers, and for 'as many as will'. Such country dances are called 'longways', with weaving *heys* through long lines of couples that Hogarth considered an excellent example of the 'S' shape being visualized in art. Actors may be asked to reconstruct historical choreographies that match the date of a play, as dances were sometimes created for a particular occasion. Research into the background of why a dance was created may give information that can be used to interpret the choreography. As Dance Consultant at the National Theatre on the production of *She Stoops to Conquer*, I taught the actors a country dance called 'The Happy Pair' because the publication date of 1755 was relevant to a very specific story. It was created for the 'coming of age' of the first Earl of Spencer who, at the ball for his 21st birthday, secretly got married in his mother's dressing room at Althorp Palace. As the first couple separated down the line, weaving between the other dancers, it was possible to construct an imagined narrative of how the lovers may have moved up the staircase, offering their hands in marriage as they join hands in the actual dance. The other dancers following the same patterns could be imagined as those dancers continuing to dance downstairs in the ballroom, maybe passing on the news between gossiping couples as they themselves move down the line.

Linking certain dance forms to specific historical figures can give the dance a dramatic context. For example, for a performance at Hampton Court Palace focusing on the Glorious Revolution of 1688, I choreographed a stately minuet to represent King William of Orange to contrast with a spritely dance to portray his wife, Queen Mary. These dance forms matched the descriptions of how the two ruling monarchs behaved in public, according to commentary by the famous diarist, John Evelyn.

Caricature and *Commedia*

Hogarth's *Analysis of Beauty* illustration of a country dance in action shows many different body shapes and sizes involved in the longways dance, with each character interpreting the dancing master's instructions in their own way. A set choreography can be presented theatrically with actors doing the same dance but using their own way of moving in character. To create this, the idea from Laban's three planes can be taken into three-dimensional moving bodies: an actor emphasizing the vertical may become a 'pin-like' figure, while an actor who takes on more horizontal movement becomes a 'wall'. An actor with extreme circular motions may appear as round as a 'ball'. All three types may then meet during the dance, maintaining their movement modes. Such an approach brings us into the realm of caricature, and the eighteenth century would not be complete without mention of pantomimic depictions in dance. Italian *commedia del'arte* theatre companies had influenced French comedy, and danced interludes were popular on the London stage. In dance terms, these characters would perform in a 'grotesque' way, using the 'false positions', so that the first good position with the toes turned out would be made in reverse, with toes facing in. This would be applied to the other positions, and the arm ornamentation could also take on asymmetric gestures. Hogarth himself notes how physical comedy is created by the contrast to noble curves made in the serpentine way, and he describes how each *commedia* character has a distinct style.

Once a noble dance has been learnt, actors may be set the challenge to turn everything inside-out, using the same choreography but substituting these 'grotesque' attitudes and false positions, even wearing *commedia* masks to become a particular character.

The paintings of Jean-Antoine Watteau and his followers depicted some dances in pastoral scenes, called the *fêtes galantes*. Noble couples aspired to the aesthetic qualities of baroque dance, but these paintings also feature Italian players and their particular poses. They exist side by side, sharing the same baroque dance vocabulary to present different characters. Dancing masters themselves are also caricatured in the art of this period, presented as stepping too high on their toes and making flamboyant gestures, in contrast to the low-life characters in Hogarth's London, for example. As the dance style becomes complex in technique, there is a danger that actors will forget the character performing the dance, or that they become so self-obsessed with their own technique that they neglect their skills in working with partners and in a group. Baroque technique became the basis for training the professional dancer. The actor may desire to gain more virtuosic skills, but should always remember that the dance belongs to a dramatic scenario.

Summary: Ornamentation and Display

The style we have been considering in this chapter requires many precise minute separate elements to be combined in a seemingly fluid whole. Each part may need to be explored separately and practised technically as a particular ornament, before being joined into the holistic combined display. The checklist below may help to keep all the separate things in mind.

Expressive Dance

Heel stepping.

1 Toe stepping.
2 Sinking and rising.
3 Mirror patterns: on the floor and with the body.
4 Upper body shaping: making the S with ornamented gestures.

Historical Dance

1 *Mouvement* – sink and rise before each step.
2 *Demi-coupé* and *pas de bourrée / fleuret* – bending and rising into single or double.
3 Positioning the feet – five good and five false positions relating to central axis.
4 *Equilibrium* – balancing on the toe with the heels together.
5 Arm Ornamentation – opposition with the feet.
6 Minuet step combining *demi-coupé* and *fleuret* (single step followed by a double step).

7 Giving hands – single and double.

8 Measuring space with the minuet step – the Z figure.

9 *Contretemps* step – hopping with gesture.

10 *Jeté* step – bending and springing forward.

Laban Dance

1 Symmetry in Space – floor patterns and baroque shapes.

2 Gesture and Posture – placements with the heel and toe.

3 Vertical Axis – move down to travel upwards.

4 *Equilibrium* – balancing the body on a central axis.

5 Arm and leg coordination – between the axis line in the body.

6 Meeting on different planes – arm gestures and body shape.

   i Arriving at the Door of Adoration.

   ii Meeting at the Table of Benediction.

   iii Bowing through the Wheel of Submission.

7 Laban includes the minuet as a dance to study as part of *Choreographie* (1926) in order to explore how the body can emphasize moving in different architectural planes.

Show Dance

1 Court dance display – show reverence in different directions.

2 Balanced patterns and step rhythms – punctuate musical phrases.

3 Male and female couple dance symmetry – baroque floor patterns.

4 Alternating between male and female steps and choreographic structures.

5 Turning the noble dance to the grotesque dance of a *commedia del'arte* character.

As an actor, try to consider how each distinct ornamental element can be used to communicate something very particular, and remember the sensation and feeling you have when you connect these separate elements to your own way of moving as one body. You may find that to reach the level where you can appear as natural as possible in this complex dance style will actually require a lot of artifice!

Further Research Springboard

- Text:
  - Soame Jenyn's poem of 1729, entitled 'The Art of Dancing', captures the way different dances were performed in England, both in the ballroom and as pastoral country dances. Characters are identified by how they behave socially on the dance floor, using their fans as a language to communicate between couples.

- Image:
  - Paintings of the king dancing:
  - Louis XIV as Apollo, 1653 (Henri Gissey).
  - Charles II in the Hague, c. 1660 (Hieronymus Janssens).
  - William Hogarth captures the new fashions and style of wearing the clothing in his caricatures and dance illustrations:
    - *The Rake's Progress*, *The Levee*, 1733.
    - *The Analysis of Beauty*, 1753.

- Music:
  - The music of Henry Purcell for the theatre is based on baroque dance rhythms, and many of these short incidental pieces can be explored with different step patterns from the Historical Dance repertoire.
  - Johann Sebastian Bach's minuets can be used to inspire a delicacy, stepping to the precise sounds of the harpsichord strings.
  - George Frederic Handel's operatic music can be used to develop fantastical characters through movement. The music styles in his masque *Acis and Galatea* to the text by John Gay clearly replicate the movement of each mythical character. For example, the entrance of the ogre Polyphemus can be interpreted by actors performing as a chorus, alternating between dramatic gestures and postures in a baroque style.

6
NINETEENTH-CENTURY COUPLING: PARTNERS PLEASE

Hoops are no more, and petticoats not much;
Morals and minuets, virtue and her stays,
And tell-tale powder – all have had their days.

LORD BYRON,
THE WALTZ, 1813

Within the Time Frame

- Empires and nations are considered as having identifiable styles, with roots in the folklore of the country.
- Ballrooms increase in size and require many couples to revolve at the same time, dancing continuously until the music ends.
- Orchestras play music with identifiable rhythms alternating different social dances for large groups of dancers, with a published programme of set dances printed on a dance card for each ball.
- Dances are organized as part of the social season, and preparation for the ball includes learning set dances and being familiar with dance tunes and correct figures appropriate for each dance.
- Codified behaviour, etiquette and styles of clothing become important social indicators in the ballroom.

An Actor Prepares to ...

- Dance face to face with partners in a ballroom hold.
- Share the same space as the partner, and step into their personal space while dancing.
- Maintain a step pattern with dancing feet while weaving arms together.
- Negotiate other moving bodies while dancing in the same space.

- Share a technique for working as a closed couple, communicating how much to turn in space and how far to travel with travelling steps.

- Use different rhythmic qualities with different dance styles, and vary the way the feet make contact with the floor.

- Improvise figures together with a partner and sense alternative rhythms within the basic underlying musical structure, while adding to the variations in the musical score.

Closed-Couple Formations

Having focused so much in this book on self-display, and keeping one's place in formation dances, this chapter will move towards an intimacy where two people must dance as one, in a closed-couple formation. The learning of couple dances from the nineteenth century will bring actors much closer to each other, quite literally. While turning together as one united pair, stepping always to one repetitive rhythm, and allowing the arms to intertwine around the partner's body, an actor must now feel completely connected to another moving body. Only when both partners are in perfect synchronization can the dance work as one moving organism. The actor needs to work very closely with someone to achieve the desired effect, so this is partner work that must be explored together, literally in the arms of another actor.

Historically, it is no wonder then that the introduction of the new face-to-face ballroom hold was commented upon by prudish polite society, which had been so used to the courtly side-by-side position. Outward show could never be entirely forgotten in a side-by-side position. In these closed-hold ballroom couple dances, each partner may become completely focused on the person they are dancing with.

The poet Lord Byron imagined how a country gentleman would react when arriving at a London ball expecting to dance the usual country dances, but instead finding the new fashion of 'valtzing' or 'waltzing' in full swing. The character, Horace Hornem, is initially shocked by the way men and women are so intertwined in each other's arms, with even his own wife, Mrs H., groping the loins of a 'hussar-looking gentleman'. He likens the constant turning of the dancing to 'two cock-chafers spitted on the same bodkin', which nowadays we may interpret as two beetles skewered by one needle, still alive and madly going round and round. Lord Byron had a reputation for being rather decadent himself, fascinated by the libertine character of Don Juan, so he cheekily imagines his fictional Mr Hornem being converted to this style of dance very quickly, and has him make a confession that he soon practises 'waltzing' regularly with his wife's maid, clearly making reference to the immoral activities that some believed 'round dancing' could inevitably lead to. The *Apostrophic Hymn to the Waltz* that Byron writes is then attributed to this Mr Hornem. It is a good description of how a new way of dancing could suddenly get many followers, almost as a new religion, being danced in so many different parts of society and spreading beyond national boundaries. Whatever social constructs people set up as barriers to protect themselves in public, insisting on polite etiquette and formal rules, once the partners are 'waltzing', the face-to-face situation gave people an intimacy where very private communication could take place much more easily.

'Waltzing' was a dance term that simply could mean turning. *A Description of the Correct Method of Waltzing* by Thomas Wilson, in 1816, is one of the earliest treatises on this dance form in England and includes waltzing to different counts of music, with the arms of the two partners linked in different poses. These poses are inherited from the 'allemanding' technique established in eighteenth-century assembly rooms. Exploring some of these positions for the arms and stringing them together into a sequence is an excellent and fun way for actors to practise physically interacting while on the move in dance.

The allemanding was considered a non-reglé dance, meaning not regulated and therefore in some way improvised, so that any of the particular arm holds could be performed in any order. By experimenting with ways of moving into different intertwined positions, using a one-hand hold, or two, both crossed over and open, techniques can be established so that the two dancers both know what move is coming next. Practising slowly may be necessary to work out which direction each person should go under which arms, so the mechanics of the moves can be understood. Eventually the change from one to another should be as fluid as possible. Even if a sequence of these moves becomes a set sequence, it should still have the feeling of spontaneity, with a constant flowing from one shape to the next. It is useful to attempt to dance these figures in different orders, finding ways of suggesting the next move to your partners by how hands are offered and what signals are given by touch.

To make these moves fluid, it is necessary to reduce tension in the hands as much as possible, so that clear direction can be given in a gentle way by turning the hand, which is then translated into the turning of the body. Using force or resisting by becoming rigid will not help the situation. The dancers must let the shape materialize gradually, with the leader of the move holding the image in his head of the intended shape that he hopes his hand signal will produce. I say 'he', as it is traditional that the gentleman would have the prerogative to decide the next move. However, he must be ready to adapt if the partner interprets the lead differently and goes in an unexpected direction. If this happens, the response may need to allow another position to materialize. There are no rules as to what figure must be used, but there must be a constant flow of shapes, and you must not stop abruptly.

Changing hands from one to the other, or from an open two-hand hold to a crossed position, also needs to be made in a fluid way. This may be made more easily with a sway forwards and backwards, to pull away and then release the finger-tips before returning to a new hold. Swaying with the music with the whole body is necessary, and the feet will keep a simple step underneath, moving all the time. This may be a triplet, as in a simple waltz step, or if in duple-time, a lilting step with moments of rising and falling of the body. There were many different rhythms for the term 'waltzing', although the three-count waltz became the most popular. While practising, it is advisable to keep some stepping all the time, even when figures go awry, so that the allemanding can keep flowing until the desired shape is found in the end.

Byron's image of two beetles skewered on one pin relates to the requirement that the partners face each other and dance around a shared central axis. They should also rotate around the room. The anticlockwise line of dance should be followed as all the couples revolve in the same direction. The simplest way to do this is to promenade: to walk in step with the arms held in one of the positions. This can be developed so that the partners also move to be at different sides of each other, making moves in front or behind, under arms and turning in and out, but always keeping an awareness of travelling on the track around the room.

Nonsuch Dance Reconstruction (16)
Allemanding

Reconstruction: Nonsuch Dances of the Courts of Europe, Volume VII.

Bow and Curtsy: Neat Feet and Tiny Inclinations

The gentleman's bow and the lady's curtsy initiate the hand hold. If this occurs at the side of the ballroom, then they bring themselves onto the dance floor either by hands joined, or the arms linked. The gentleman may simply step forward and make a small bend from the waist. The lady makes a small curtsy in response. In the Regency period, when the dresses revealed the lady's ankle and feet, the placement of the feet had to be precise: for example, with the third position, the heel should touch the instep, and when making a curtsy from the side she may step from a second position to the fourth position, before bending. Bending in a fourth position may deepen the curtsy, which becomes necessary as the circular shape of the dress expands in the course of the century. The gentleman maintains the feet together, or in a small second position, and respect is shown with the head bowing and inclining from the waist.

Litheness and Lightness

Although *allemanding* dancing began life in the eighteenth century, the moves can be executed even more freely in the lighter clothing of the Regency period. The couple are able to be in closer proximity now that the ladies' dresses cling to their waists. Their long gloves emphasized the full arm revealed to the shoulder.

Regular Step Pattern

The Music continues with a regular repeating rhythm. In the Nonsuch Dance Reconstruction, a lilting step is used when possible to fit the duple-time music, with a clear accent on the first beat. The actual steps are not important at this stage, providing the partners can keep moving together.

Forward or Backward Motions with Turns

Moving forward and backward is possible with one or two hands linked. The hands may be lifted high when the dancers meet on the forward step taken on a rise of the foot. These hand positions do act as a barrier to prevent the couple getting too close while dancing in public! The turn under the arm requires that the arms and hands are relaxed: the gentleman lifts his arm and as the lady has moved under his arm, he faces her again on the opposite side.

Hiding the Hands

Both partners always need to have their free hands ready to make a new connection that will need to occur at the end of one move and lead into the next without a break in the rhythmic flow. The changing of hands is made as part of the releasing moment of one sequence. The less the onlookers notice this change of hand the better, so this move is preferred as a low handhold that is lifted up again on the next move.

From a two-hand hold, it can be changed from open to closed, as partners meet on a forward motion: as the hands are close to the body, the change is partially hidden from the onlookers, so the illusion of hands seamlessly changing and interweaving may be achieved.

Promenading with Turns: Continuing the Line of Dance

The hands are lightly touching so that the ladies' hands are free enough to turn. This is important as the gentleman lifts the hands high. For both the one-hand or two-hand promenade, the hands may be in a crossed or open position in front of the body.

Interlocking into a 'Window' Figure: Precision Without Tension

Two hands are linked in crossed formation. The hands must be as lightly touching as possible, but the turning motion must be continually made by the man's hands. The lady turns under the two linked hands. She makes two turns and on the second turn she allows her body to twist so they are both side by side, with the shoulders touching. The gentleman lowers the arm that is now inside the shape, so that the 'window' frame is made.

Turning in and out: Constant Flow

The moves where one partner comes into the side of the other, or behind each other, need to be practised to achieve a balanced flow between each partner, with moments of slight suspension where they catch a glimpse of each other in the new position. It has a rolling see-saw sensation.

The *Allemande* Hold

This is a completely intertwined position with the couple revolving side by side, facing the direction they are travelling, with their arms linked behind their backs.

This hold does not begin with holding hands. Instead it begins with the free hands coming together as if to shake hands, but not connecting until they have passed under the arm of the partner, almost as if to do a swing of the arms, and then resting on the back of the partner. The other hand will then be placed behind the back to take hold and complete the position. To release from this hold, the arms are pulled from behind the partner's back. As the arms are coming away, these hands can join. The other hands can then link to make a crossed two-hand hold.

The Bower

This position wraps the lady into the man's side, with his hand around her waist, and both of their other arms raised, making a curved arch over their heads. From an open two-hand hold, one hand moves in front of the body and upwards as the other arm remains at waist level. This final position has been poetically named *the bower* as the shape represents an arbour sheltering the couple. Waltzing could continue for many revolutions in this hold, which demonstrates the potential intimacy of this type of dance.

A Motto for Rehearsing Allemanding

Explore and experiment, find what works for you.
Then repeat many times – till it's easy to do.

Nineteenth-Century National Identities

The couple dances in vogue in ballrooms from the mid-nineteenth century period have connections to different nationalities. The opening of the formal balls in the capital cities of Europe was a grand occasion for dignitaries, titles, uniforms, medals and badges of distinction to be shown off, as couples lined up for the Grand March or the *Polonaise* dance.

The March demanded stately stepping to the duple-time rhythm, such as with the famous *Radetzky March* composed in 1848, dedicated to Austrian Field Marshal Joseph Radetzky von Radetz, composed by Johann Strauss I.

The Strauss Family

Johann Strauss I was a great composer of dance music for the period, leading dance bands in Vienna. His son, Johann Strauss II, became internationally more famous as 'The Waltz King'. The popular dance rhythms were played with different speeds, adding pauses as suspended musical moments. His most famous Viennese Waltz, *The Waltz of the Blue Danube*, is a good example of this innovation.

Marching Warm-Up

A Grand March such as *The Radetzky March* gets people clapping and stamping their feet to the strong beats. This order and regularity gave the uplift needed to get any big occasion off the ground, and still serves the same purpose when played as part of the 'Last Night of the Proms' with the audience in London's Royal Albert Hall clapping the very strong beats. A great warm-up for dancing in this period could encourage stepping out every beat with military-style marching.

Processional *Polonaise*

The *Polonaise* may be a little less familiar, as this Polish processional dance employs the triple rhythm, but the stepping will still need to accent to the first beat. This is a good warm-up for stepping with three clear beats. While stepping to *Polonaise* music, emphasize the first beat by stepping further forward, so the stretch gives more power to the first step. This dance is for couples to process around the room, so all the types of formations from other periods which use lines, couples and groups could be used, making arches, following leaders into formations, and lines coming forward to the front to appear majestic. The gentleman may even have one arm raised above his lady, making a very clear statement expressing a grand arrival triumphing into the space, as used in the opening of the *mazurka* on the dance reconstruction.

Contrasting Couple Dances

The 'Light-Footed' Polka *and the* 'Heavy-Stamped' Mazurka

The Dance Reconstruction has samples of two dances that present different flavours of couple dance from the nineteenth-century ballroom. The *polka* is noted for the light hopping which elevates the bodies as the couples turn, suited to what Laban may categorize as 'high movers' who prefer to move in the upper level, staying up and away from the floor while dancing. In contrast, the *mazurka* requires the feet to have contact with the floor whenever possible, with gliding, thrusting and stamping steps suited to the 'low movers' of Laban Dance who enjoy moving in the lower level, where even the distinctive heel kicks and hops off the ground only skim over the surface.

Dance Manuals

Written instructions for dancing as a couple at the balls in London and Paris were included in numerous etiquette books for the ballroom, sometimes directed to the men and sometimes specifically to the ladies. Translations and adaptations inspired several other versions that were published in the USA. One such American manual of 1856 by Charles Durang is entitled *The Fashionable Dancer's Casket or the Ballroom Instructor, a new and splendid work on Dancing, Etiquette, Deportment and the Toilet.* In this period, the word 'toilet' is used in reference to the attire worn for the event, and the first chapter addresses the way to dress. This is advice taken directly from the etiquette manual written by Mrs Henderson of London. Durang states that:

> It is the fashion at present to wear long dresses: but in having the dresses thus made, orders should be given not to have them so long as they touch the ground: for in that case they are apt to be torn before half the evening is over. It is almost impossible to thread the mazes of the dance without such an accident. (p. 13)

The guests needed advice on how to survive in a ballroom with so many couples dancing all together on the dance floor.

Illustrations in the manual show couples wearing the fashion of the ballroom, with full-skirted gowns for the ladies and tailored suits for the gentleman. When giving instructions for the *mazurka*, however, it is worth noting that the accompanying picture depicts dancers in folk costume, dancing in boots. The roots of these national dances are imagined to lead back to a particular group of people, a 'folk', who found personal expression in that particular dance form. Of course, once we are in the highly polished ballrooms of polite high society, any such folk-dancing boots must be removed and replaced with the ballroom shoe, which was a very light slipper, making it possible to glide the foot along the floor. Likewise, the folk steps were modified to match the fashion. It is useful for actors, however, to identify a residue of this earthy style in the later cultured form. Actors may wish to emphasize this to give a particular texture to the dance, displaying a characteristic flavour, even if they must refrain from stamping their boots as noisily. To get the feel of each national dance, it is worth the actor looking at what elements contribute to this folkloristic representation, and what made it link to a particular place and time.

Nonsuch Dance Reconstruction (17)
Mazurka

Reconstruction: Nonsuch Dances from the Courts of Europe, Volume VII.

Digging up the Roots

This image of a 'folk dance' can be maintained when considering the *mazurka* dance: the historical dance of the *mazurs* – the men who lived in the plains of Mazovia, around Warsaw. This dance in triple rhythm uses a combination of different accented steps, strong steps into the ground, stamping and clicking of the heels. There are illustrations of men dancing this dance with stirrups on their heavy boots, with women also booted and in working aprons, both partners with sashes tied around their waist seemingly flowing wildly with the motion. It is a matter of debate as to how authentic these visual depictions were of the people who actually lived in these regions, but during this period of patriotism there were many paintings of such traditional costumes used to signify different nations.

By 1849 in London, the *mazurka* was included in the published collection of *Fashionable Dances,* which was a translation of Henri Cellarius' *Danses des Salons*, published in Paris a few years earlier. The dance is noted for its particular energy and style:

> Of all the new dances which have been introduced of late … there is none, perhaps, whose character is more marked with spirit and originality than the Mazurka … The Mazurka is composed at once of impulse, majesty, unreservedness, and allurement. It has something of the proud and the warlike. (Cellarius, *Fashionable Dances*, pp. 52–61)

Presentational Positions

The arrival onto the performance area, be this in a ballroom or on a stage, begins the expression of the style of the dance. The arm positions should add to the 'proud majesty', placing the hands on the hips or lifted in the air with strong poses made with extended arms. The entry prepares the onlookers for a display that will be valued by the different combinations of rhythms in the steps. Each performer makes their mark on the space with an introductory section comprising different accented steps. The steps are presented to the other partner, with the man maybe kneeling to the lady, and alternating in a game-like manner, before joining as a couple.

Ballroom Hold

The difference in height and body shape between two dancers always determines how high the man's right hand will be when placed around the lady's waist, with the left hand holding the lady's right. Cartoons in this period, such as in the satirical magazine *Punch*, give evidence of the comic potential when mismatched couples of different heights would adopt their version of a ballroom hold. Each ballroom hold would of course need to vary with the particular partner at the time. However, for actors it is important to consider the technical elements of the ballroom hold. When two actors meet to join, they should both imagine the space they are enclosing, and remember the 'active surrounding' that their bodies are involved with. It is not so much about making contact with another body, holding the waist and hand, but rather about sharing a circled space together. This circle spans around their own backs as well as around the space where their partner is placed. As the steps are introduced, it is necessary that the actors imagine they are both energizing this shape throughout. The circle space is made both from the outside curving and the volume of the empty space inside the couple being actively maintained.

Steps and Rhythms

There are a variety of steps that can be made within the *mazurka* rhythm to emphasize different stamps and accent different beats. Original Polish names were translated into French, with some alternative abbreviations. In his *Grammar of the Art of Dancing*, Friedrich Albert Zorn noted that 'perhaps the principal attraction in this singular dance lies in the fact that the dancer is at liberty to vary his steps at will' (1887, translated in Boston in 1905). Actors can explore making different combinations and inter-acting with the musical accompaniment.

Pas marché – walking step – skimming along the surface.

- Three steps with a different emphasis on each: weak, medium, strong.
- The walk may be ended with stamps in place and heel clicks.

Pas mazur – hopping step – lifting the body to slide and shunt.

- Three steps: hop, slide, shunt.
- The footing: left hop, right slide, right shunt / right hop, left slide, left shunt.
- Hop and bring the other leg in towards the ankle, slide this foot along the floor, then shunt forward on this foot with the other leg extending to the back. This extended leg moves from back to the front to join the ankle, as the supporting foot hops, before the back leg slides forward once more.

Pas corru – running step – travelling with leaps forward.

- Travelling steps stay low to the ground, with stamps as the foot skims the surface.
- A small jump at the end of the three steps emphasizes the moment of arrival.

Pas mazur promenade – skating step – gliding side by side.

- In a side-by-side formation, the 'skating' handhold also adds to the gliding sensation.
- Three steps: walking steps can be used.
- Transition: *allemanding* after the revolve to prepare for the ballroom hold position.

Pas gala – sliding step – sliding feet together as a couple.

- Three steps: slide, step, hop.
- Footing: left slide / right step / right hop. Continues on the same footing.
- The outward foot slides forward, the other foot joins from behind, the back foot hops so that the front foot is lifted ready to begin the sequence again.
- Transition: the three-count waltz turn can be used to add contrast with some smooth gliding.

Holubéc / Coup de talon – heel clicks – jumping together as a couple.

- Beat the heels and then make two steps (beat, step, step).
- This can be made to be virtuosic with many more heel hits in a continuous sequence one after each other.
- These steps may be used for solo display.

Port de bras – presentation of arms

- When revolving, lift the arms to join at the top, using *allemanding* figures, and ending in a proud presentational stance.

Nonsuch Dance Reconstruction (18) *Polka*

Reconstruction: Nonsuch Dances from the Courts of Europe, Volume VII.

Imaginative Histories

By the middle of the nineteenth century the *polka* had become a dance craze, featured in all the ballrooms in Europe. People questioned where it had come from. Historical research into the period can help an actor imagine the occasion where the dance appeared, but it is also a worthwhile exercise to consider some of the stories and myths surrounding the dance itself. Exploring these ideas in a physical way may mean that the actor engages even more with the story of the dance in the context of the people of the time. There is more to it than simply moving the feet in a particular way. If dance history can help actors understand why it was popular at that time, they may connect with the personalities of the people who influenced the very character of the dance.

The *polka* is ideal for this type of imaginative historical approach. There are many stories and theories about where the *polka* may have come from, and how the dance travelled before arriving into high society, when it would be written down and published in manuals.

In June 1844, when the *polka* was at the height of its fashion, the national newspaper *Bohemia* asked the respected Czech historian Zibrt to publish his history of the origins of the *polka* dance. He wanted to make sure that the *polka* remained part of Czech national history, so he gave a very detailed account of all the people involved. I will give the outline of the history he proposed, and suggest how actors can then be inspired creatively in the studio from this scenario and produce versions of a 'polka' that suit different situations.

The following scenario can be 'put on its feet' by actors in the studio, acting the scenario with improvised spoken exchanges between the characters, and considering how to create the movement styles best suited for each situation, to give each scene a different *polka* style.

Scene 1: Little Anna Arrives – 'Getting to Know You!'

It is 1834, in a small town in central Bohemia called Kostelec ned Labem. A young girl called Anna Chadimova arrives. She has travelled a fair distance from her small village to find work. She meets the important Klastersky family. She is offered work as a serving-maid to the family. Anna is so pleased to have been given a job, she sings a folk song and dances as she works:

'Uncle Nimra Bought a White Horse' sings Anna.
'What is that you are doing?' asked the children.
'*Madera*' says Anna, which means 'something happy and lively' in her dialect.

Expressive Dance

- Create the scene where Anna meets the family, and begins work, and makes up her lively song and dance while also doing her tasks around the house.
- Suggested words: childlike, lively, little hops.
- Lightly dusting while jumping in the air.

Scene 2: The Music Lesson – 'Hello Young Lovers!'

The music teacher, Josef Neruda, arrives to teach the children the piano. Josef is enthralled as he sees Anna singing and dancing. He writes down the simple tune and composes a version for Anna to dance to.

Expressive Dance

- Create the scene where Josef is fascinated with Anna.
- Create the dance she does for him.
- Create the version when he plays the music and she dances.
- Suggested words: playful, flirtatious, precocious, provocative.
- Use of the skirt while dancing.

Scene 3: The Tavern – 'Roll Out the Barrel!'

The music teacher Josef Neruda is so pleased with his composition that he plays the tune in the taverns. Men sing and dance while drinking Czech beer, and the women join in. Soon the whole town is dancing to the new tune.

Expressive Dance

- Create the scene in the tavern, and the dance that the men do in their inebriated way.
- Imagine dancing this with the women, then into the streets.
- Suggested words: wild, raucous, swaying, reeling, many turns.
- Use of the heel and toe, Bohemian style.

Scene 4: From Prague to Vienna to Paris, 1835–40 – 'Shall We Dance?'

Our historian now tells us that the music journeys from Prague to Vienna and finally Paris, being played first by the small dance bands and then the orchestras, increasing in size for the larger ballrooms. In 1840, the famous Prague dancing master, named Raab, is invited to dance at the Odeon Theatre in Paris, and the dance is a hit with the French dancing masters, including the celebrated Henri Cellarius, who includes the dance in his instruction manual of 1847, *La danse de salon*.

Expressive Dance

- Create the feeling of dancing to the nineteenth-century orchestra, and how this might alter the dance style in a grand ballroom.
- Create a form of the dance that might be performed as a theatre dance for a fashionable Parisian audience.
- Create a form of the dance that might be taught as a ballroom dance, sliding the feet along the polished dance floors, and wearing soft ballroom slippers.
- Suggested words: refined, gliding the feet, making light and small hops from the floor, placing the feet close to the ankle on the hop.

Epilogue: What we Have Learnt from Anna

We have come a long way from the Little Anna of the small Czech town, whose real name we have probably forgotten, but we could believe that the elements of that childlike fun are still there somewhere in the dance. Of course, having now worked through this narrative in a creative way, inspiring the imagination with so many locations and personalities, it may be that the simplest idea of the dance being a turning dance with a half step hop (*pulka* meaning 'cut in half' in Czech) is just much too simple to comprehend! Indeed, even this historically reconstructed dance is also a long way from the stilted polka that schoolteacher Anna will try to teach the King of Siam in the Hollywood film musical *The King and I*, singing 'Shall We Dance: 1, 2, 3, and …'

How to do a Half-Step Hop

The distinctive hop of the polka must be placed before the three steps take off in any direction. The ballroom dancing masters will stress the need for the other foot to come near the ankle as one foot leaves the floor. The more wild you dance the *polka* step, the more is the desire to lift the knee of the gesturing leg to show the fun of the dance, but this energy may need to be restrained. The lightness also needs to make the hop a very precise move, so that it feels as if things are being contained before the body sets off in the next direction.

- **Polka politesse:** Even the delicate hopping of the rhythm should make the encounter light and airy, offering hands and preparing for the preparatory hop to begin the rhythm.

- **Promenade forward and backward:** Hopping with the inside foot to begin stepping with the outside foot, then reverse.

- **Promenading face to face and back to back:** The outside foot steps forward, bringing partners to face each other. The inside foot comes forward, turning the partners away from each other. The hands are lightly held so that arms move forward and backward.

- **Polka turns:** Two polka steps complete the turn of the couple around the line of dance.

- **Promenade open:** You may alternate between open positions and ballroom hold.

- **Bohemian heel and toe:** Use the outside foot to dig the heel into the ground, then pull back to place on the toe before the supporting leg makes a preparatory hop for a sidewards polka step. Return against the line of dance with the other foot making the heel-toe gesture.

- **Finale polka turns:** As the couple travel with more energy they may travel over more distance. The moment of the hop is used for the man to consider what space is available to travel as a couple. All dancers may be travelling in the same direction around the ballroom, but not necessarily covering the same amount of ground, so the note about avoiding accidents becomes very relevant here!

Filling the Dance Card

A typical ball during the nineteenth century would alternate between group dances and couple dances. So the social situation would alternate between dancing with partners and then back to being in larger groups, which would involve more public display. Group dances developed from the established country dance formations and popular *longways* country dances where dancers were divided into smaller sets of two or three couples (duple or triple minor sets) moving up the line, giving opportunities to meet new people. Dancing in a square formation made of four couples became established from the eighteenth century. First, this was the French *cotillion*: a favourite of the English novelist Jane Austen, who even copies down the music to the *Rose Cotillion* in her notebook. From this dance developed the quadrille, with a more regimented choreographic structure, alternating between two couples dancing at a time, allowing the other two couples moments for conversation. The planning of who would be your partner for the many different dances of the ball could create a dramatic narrative of its own, as happens for example in the ball scenes from the novels of Jane Austen. Dance cards of the period list the order of dances and hint at the potential for drama on such occasions, deciding who would fill the gaps for named partners, and who may be left without a partner or mismatched.

Summary: Couples Working as One

Couple ballroom dances represent one style of dance that was performed on formal occasions during the nineteenth century. Exploring ways of turning in these dances and stepping the feet to the many different rhythms may be quite a hazardous exercise. Let us end with the words Lord Byron gives to Mr Hornem on 'round' dancing:

> Now that I know what it is, I like it of all things, and so does Mrs H. (though I have broken my shins, and four times overturned Mrs. Hornem's maid, in practicing the preliminary steps in a morning …)

Actors will need to persevere with their partners, so that it becomes a pleasurable experience to dance as a couple with the shared sensation of moving as one dancing entity.

Further Research Springboard

- Text:
  - Jane Austen's novels include a number of dance scenes where the anxiety of waiting for an invitation from a partner is part of the drama of the occasion. The introduction of closed couple dancing makes it important who dances which dance, when and with whom.
  - Nineteenth-century novelists such as Thomas Hardy show the social dance activity in varying locations and the social transactions conducted there. Dancing allows women direct communication with the opposite sex that would frequently be restricted in other environments.
  - Thackeray's *Vanity Fair* references the Duchess of Richmond's famous ball, held on the eve of the Battle of Waterloo.
- Image:
  - Consider how the fashion changes through the period. The silhouette of the ladies' dresses influences how dances with couples develop. The slim-line Regency empire line gradually gives way to the tight corset with voluminous crinoline skirts. This has a significant impact on where the arms are placed when in the ballroom hold, and the space required to move around the floor.
  - Notice how the footwear differs for the ballroom from other activities in the period. The waltz required the men to wear slipper-type shoes to glide along the floor and turn easily with the lady. This period also sees the move away from tight breeches and pantaloons for men, into slim fitting trousers.

- Costume images appear alongside social diary information in periodicals and journals such as in *The Ladies Monthly Museum*, the American *Ladies' Magazine* and, later in the century, *The Lady*, England's longest-running weekly magazine, first published in 1885.

- Fashions, styles and gestures in portraits can be seen in the work of Victorian artists such as Franz Xaver Winterhalter and John Singer Sargent. Robert Alexander Hillingford paints the scene of the Duchess of Richmond's Ball, and William Powell Frith's paintings show a full variety of Victorian characters such as at *Derby Day* and in *The Railway Station*.

- Music:
  - Set dance tunes:
    - Once you have become accustomed to dancing to the set rhythms of the dances, it is possible to alternate between dances in different rhythms. Compilations of nineteenth-century ballroom music will combine *mazurkas* with *polkas* and *waltzes*. Identify changes in the music and, as they share the triplet rhythm, vary how you perform steps to match the appropriate dance character. Frédéric Chopin's concert versions of *mazurkas* for solo piano are suitable for such an exercise.

  - Viennese whirling:
    - Johann Strauss II developed the waltz even further in his compositions, which he himself conducted while playing his violin, varying the speed of the pulse. Listen to Viennese waltzes such as *The Blue Danube* recorded by a full orchestra, and match your dancing to the changing speeds, as each section takes on a different pulse. Sense the moments of slowing down and then speeding up. You can do this while moving alone, maintaining a free flow in your body and using your arms to conduct the orchestra. Allow the full sound to give you confidence to become a whirling dervish, letting the wild turns support you around a central axis. You can also try exploring this joined together with a partner, finding a suspension in the body to match the moments of hesitation in the music.

7

TWENTIETH-CENTURY FOXTROTS: CRAZY DANCES AND DANCE CRAZES

P.C.Q.
(Please Charleston Quietly)

NOTICE AT THE HAMMERSMITH PALAIS DANCE HALL, 1927

Within the Time Frame

- Beginning in the carefree world of the upper class in Edwardian England (1901–11), before the sinking of the *Titanic* in 1912 and the outbreak of the First World War in 1914.

- Developing from the Ragtime era came jazz music with improvisation and syncopation.

- New dance crazes appear with the so-called 'Jazz Age' in 1920s America, ending with the Depression.

- Music hall and Vaudeville theatre influenced popular social dance.

- The fashions for the ladies gave more freedom to move, or flap their arms and legs – such young ladies became known as 'flappers'.

- Social dances appeared in a glamorous way in early cinema, with performers such as Fred Astaire beginning his career on stage on Broadway and London, before his dancing was captured in the first Hollywood musical films.

An Actor Prepares to ...

- Isolate body parts rhythmically.

- Syncopate movement and find juxtaposing rhythms.

- Break from the couple formation to perform solo.

- Caricature and mimic in a comic way.

- Use theatrical styles while still relating to partners in a social way.

- Sense a partner without touching, improvising mirrored patterns, and physically interlinking with energetic jumping sequences together.

- Move freely in wild and extreme ways in all directions.

- Develop stamina and high performance energy with fast, furious dance sequences.

'Phew, Open the Windows!'

That's what the Reverend E. W. Rogers, vicar of St Aidan's in Bristol, is supposed to have said when the Charleston craze took off in England in the 1920s. He believed that, 'Any lover of the beautiful will die rather than be associated with the Charleston. It is neurotic! It is rotten! It stinks!' (Such evidence, either supporting or criticizing different dance forms, has been collected in Frances Rust's overview entitled *Dance in Society*, published in London in 1969.)

If you have been physically exploring the dance styles so far in this book you will have worked pretty hard with your dancing body and exerted a fair amount of physical effort, but most of the instruction on etiquette for polite society in the earlier periods emphasized the need to hide this exertion and appear as if everything is effortless. This chapter focuses on the popular dances of the early twentieth century. The one that has survived in some form today is the Charleston, which is a dance that makes it very difficult to hide its inherent energy. In fact you need to display that energy outwardly to make this dance come alive as an expression of a new craze where the syncopated rhythms of jazz take over. Now we must think less of the body as a whole and instead isolate each individual body part and then shake it all about!

In actor training, we still want to develop a controlled technique and use this skill in action, but now, above all, the energy should be infectious and encourage onlookers to feel as if they, too, could jump up and join in. We still need to consider these as social dances, performed in social situations, as a recreational pursuit to meet people in the ballroom and have fun. However, even at their moment of creation, these social dances made a conscious link to dances that were being performed in spectacular shows in theatres at the time, so from the beginning they present a more theatrical form of expression. Invention is to be encouraged, as there are many variations and configurations that can be made from the material, and this can lead the actor into the world of choreography, so that the idea of structure and narrative can be used to arrange unique sequences for a solo display or demonstrate perfect synchronization with other dancers. There should be a surprise element of not knowing what will come next, and this will help keep the studio energized and build up stamina in a fun and creative way.

Ragtime Bounce

The Charleston apparently became popular in a 1923 revue called *Runnin' Wild* that toured the United States. Wildly running to the music is the easiest way to get started with this style. Let the body bounce to the ragtime rhythm, which has a one-step count, giving every beat a step or an action, and let the whole body respond to each step or move, moving around the room and adding light and fast little dabbing and flicking motions with gestures of the hands and feet, going in all the different directions. Use different parts of the body to create these isolated moves, using all the joints of the limbs, so that the body makes a variety of ever-changing angular shapes. Even when you are standing in one place, keep the bounce going. The heels and toes can lift from the floor. There are no 'true' or 'false' positions, or any need to find 'balance' or 'measure' in this expressive dance moment. Now, as a dancing star, you are electric – seemingly producing your own fast alternating current in whatever which way!

Teddy Bears' Picnic

In the Edwardian era there was a short-lived craze for dances that have been called the 'animal dances'. The Tudors may have taken the idea of the preening peacock into their majestic dance for important ceremonial display, but it was a very different style when a dancing couple would shamelessly mimic turkeys, rabbits, bears, ostriches and other creatures while doing their manic one-step bouncing. The *Bunny-Hop* allowed couples to jump side by side, the *Grizzly Bear* had partners hugging with their arms stretched wide, and the waddling of poultry inspired the *Turkey Trot*. For actors, I suggest that the rather ridiculous task of creating 'animal dances' is a worthwhile exercise for exploring hesitation and syncopation while keeping linked to the main pulse of the music.

The following exercise can be danced to any ragtime one-step music, and should be a combination of solo invention, partner work and consideration of how to perform the dance to an audience.

- Choose an animal to inspire your dance.

- Create caricatured moves for the creature: how might you step the feet and select isolated hand and arm actions? (The more comic and ridiculous the better for this style!)

- Take these gestures to the extreme while still doing a simple one-step walk or bouncing to the rhythm and produce a repetitive sequence combining all the moves.

- Find a way to connect these moves with a partner as a couple dance.

- Consider how you could use the ballroom couple-hold at certain points in the dance, and how you might revolve as a couple, travelling down the line of dance of the dance floor. You may need to adapt the steps and physical hold, but attempt to keep related to moves suitable to your own caricatured animal.

Without Hesitation

The *foxtrot* may have come into being as one of these 'animal dances' in the ballroom (as the *Fox Trot*), although the name of this dance was actually made popular by the Vaudevillian actor Harry Fox. His *foxtrot* developed into a stepping sequence combining slow and fast walking steps as a couple dance, which would remain the style for future decades of ballroom dance. In 1914 the outbreak of war sobered English society, and these comic couple dance novelties would be replaced by more serious ballroom dancing in the next decade and beyond. An international style for ballroom dance would be established with Victor Sylvester and the Imperial Society of Teachers of Dancing in the late 1920s and the hesitation created by the syncopation of ragtime would be refined to match set musical rhythms established in the 1930s.

Vaudeville Version

Using the material from the previous exercise, actors should first think how their invented animal couple dance could be presented as a vaudeville act: as a Show Dance being presented on a music-hall stage. How would the arrival of the dancers demonstrate which animal was being caricatured, and what story could be told with the actions as a short comedy routine during the dance? Piano ragtime music by Scott Joplin is a very suitable accompaniment for such a comic routine.

Sombre Stepping

Then a more refined version of the dance can be created, as a couple dance appearing more sober, sombre and stylish, with consideration as to when to make quick or slow steps. The stepping should then be organized so that the couple can progress around the room – alternating who walks forward and who takes backward steps, and how to turn together as a couple. As a competitive ballroom dance, consider when the moments of hesitation can be used to acknowledge the onlookers, and consider how the dance can still display the harmony between the two dancers with synchronized steps and arm gestures. The same dance moves can be varied to different stepping rhythms that match the music of ballroom tango, waltz or foxtrot.

The *Shostakovich Jazz Suites* offer versions of these dance rhythms that have a clear pulse with syncopations in the orchestration, so that the one-step idea can be developed into an elegant ballroom dance while keeping the fun of the animal caricatures.

Creative Competition

The ballroom and the stage were sharing ideas when it came to the Charleston. Solo performers such as Josephine Barker would add virtuosic kicks and rotation of limbs, creating steps such as 'donkey kicks' and the 'monkey knees' with manic poses such as 'the scarecrow'. Couples may dance together, sometimes in ballroom hold, while bouncing and kicking in unison, or separating from each other to perform solo variations or combined choreographic sequences which were synchronized together.

Competitions in the Charleston became popular in London, such as at the highly prestigious Charleston Ball in Piccadilly in 1926, with prizes offered to both professional and amateur categories, presented on this occasion by the dance celebrity Fred Astaire. Competitiveness can make actors work even harder. Moves can be fitted to the Charleston rhythm that are impressive to watch and demonstrate technical skill, with maybe high kicks and rotation of isolated limbs, and fast changes of direction. Performers may find ways to entertain by including a narrative connected to the relationship between other dancers, or dancing as a synchronized couple with a slickly choreographed routine, or performing a solo engaging directly with the audience. When asked the secret to making his dance look so natural, Fred Astaire is supposed to have said, 'I just put my feet in the air and move them about!' We all know that it is never as simple as that, but that is a good way to begin inventing a crazy Charleston dance which makes an audience smile at the novelty of the gestures or be impressed with how moves are made energetically from one step to another. In the filmed sample you will find a number of steps that I hope will inspire your own versions, and help produce a final 'Show Dance-off' to 'show off' your dancing skills.

Charleston Basic: The Step-Touch

The basic step pattern of making one step and then one gesture of the other leg will give the basic 'step-touch' rhythm.

- This alternates between forward and backward steps.
- Step forward with one foot, placing the weight onto this leg; then let the other leg, go forward and touch the floor ahead.
- This gesturing foot then steps back behind the supporting leg to take the weight of the body, and the first foot can then be released to gesture towards the back, touching the floor at the back, before beginning the sequence again.

It is useful to practise the step-touch pattern to Charleston music and then add the bounce, so that the upper body moves constantly with the stepping. The arms can then gesture as the feet move. The gesturing leg can become a kick in different directions, and the arms can work in opposition, and isolation from other body parts can then be added to this basic.

Rotation of the Knees

The Charleston instruction manuals tell us how the knees should rotate throughout the stepping sequence, so that each foot is swivelling as it makes a step and the gesturing leg also rotates. Start with your heels together in a first position. As you lift both heels, let your knees come together so that your heels move away. Then return as the knees come back to the first position. This rotation on both legs will continue as one leg steps and the other makes the gesture. It takes practice to keep such a motion going throughout the sequence, and of course there is potential strain on the knee-joints – contemporary critics noted this to be one of the health hazards of too much Charleston dancing. As with all new ways of stepping in dance, it is advisable to begin gently and not get too carried away too soon: it is still possible to do the basic steps and gestures without having to rotate the knees beyond what feels comfortable.

The Flapper Finale

The flapper costume allows complete freedom for the legs to kick and the arms to move freely. The lightness of the fabric allows the dress to move with the constant bouncing motion in this style: this may be emphasized with tassels added as trimming. Headbands may have feathers attached, and beads can be worn and used as props in the choreography. The gentleman in his eveningwear can take on a suave and sophisticated style. Dressed in black and white, imagine moving in the speeded up silent movies and let the perspiration make you glow like an electric light bulb!

Nonsuch Dance Reconstruction (19)
Charleston

Reconstruction: Nonsuch Dancers for the MOVE IT exhibition, Olympia, London, 2012.

Solo Side-by-Side Opening

Arriving to begin the Charleston.

Charleston Chase

Lightly running with a bounce, bending the knee joints. The arms may be held by the sides, with the characteristic isolation of the wrists.

Side Shunts

Keep the feet together and shunt forward and backward on each beat. The arms may rise together, with isolation from the elbows. There may be little bounces when the feet are together.

Charleston Basic

The step-touch combination. Arms may move forward and backward in a wild swinging style, emphasizing isolation from the shoulders.

Partner Charleston

The dancers can join by running to meet in ballroom hold, and stay united as a couple.

Chase with Bounce-Kicks

The man moves forward, backing the lady with four steps, counting 1, 2, 3, 4. The couple then bounces with feet together before isolating from the knee and kicking one foot to the back. The couple need to decide which leg will kick back. If the dance is being directed to one designated front, then it is usual to start with the 'downstage' leg for the first sequence, as that is the leg more prominently on view and makes the first kick more visible:

5 Bounce

6 Kick back

7 Bounce

8 Kick back

To repeat, both the direction and footing alternates, so the lady moves forward, the man moves back, and the opposite 'upstage' legs are used for the kicks.

Basic in Partner Hold

The lady begins by stepping back as the man steps forward, to make the step-touch basic.

Charleston Chase in a Circle

Still in couple formation, they can rotate making their own circle.

Side Shunts as a Couple

The shunting step goes to either side of the partner.

Charleston Chase to Release

The running step can be used to open back to solo positions.

Presentational Charleston Moves

Heel Hits

As the leg kicks to the side, the same hand hits the heel. These can be on the same leg or alternate, and used while turning on the spot. The other arm can be raised and isolating the hand gesture.

Aeroplane Arms

While the arms remain outstretched they can move as aeroplane wings dropping to one side and then the other. The feet can kick the heels to meet the hand, going outside and away from the body, or inside and crossing the body. The crossing leg may go in front or behind the other leg, but must meet the hand that is coming down to the appropriate side. This is a good step to train coordination of moving arms and legs together.

Table 7.1: Leg / Arm Coordination of Aeroplane Arms

Leg direction	Hand hits the heel	Aeroplane arm dropping directions Right–Left alternation
Right leg open to side	Outside	Right hand hits heel
Right leg crossing in front supporting leg	Inside	Left hand hits heel
Left leg crossing supporting leg (either behind or in front)	Inside	Right hand hits heel
Left leg open to side	Outside	Left hand hits heel

The aeroplane arms may be changed to a left–right direction, in which case the leg direction would also be changed.

Scarecrow

The hands and feet are pulled outwards by a feeling of the shoulders being strung up as the elbows are isolated and lifted upwards.

Monkey Knees

The knees open and close, while the hands placed on the knees switch from having arms crossed and then open again.

Concluding Variations

The dancer can move around in a circle, placing the step of the basic step in a different direction. The basic step can be varied by allowing the gesturing leg to kick, and adding extra little kicks of the feet in the air to the half-beats of the music. A kick behind may become a wild 'donkey kick', and heel hits can be added to kicks at the front or behind. Kicks forward may get higher with the Charleston basic, and end with an open presentational position, with every finger isolated, producing the characteristic 'jazz hands'.

Summary: Isolating Body Parts

How crazy can a dance craze be? Crazy animal-type dances seem to have had short-lived moments in many centuries. Even in 2013, dance moves based on riding a horse became viral when the singer Psy produced his Gangnam style music video. Even this endless sequence of repeated moves can be made dramatic if we connect with the reasons why people are enjoying this activity, and connect the choreography to the characters of those copying this trend. As you step into a different dance dimension, always be aware of how you can isolate your energy to emphasize very specific stylistic choices and make sure you give precise focus to your every move – even in this hyper-manic mode of exhilarated ecstasy.

Further Research Springboard

- Text:
    - A view of Edwardian England can be read in E. M. Forster's novel *Maurice*, written in 1913–14, which addresses the changes occurring in twentieth-century society before the First World War.
    - The novelist F. Scott Fitzgerald captures the speed of the 1920s in works such as *The Beautiful and the Damned* and *The Great Gatsby*.
- Image:
    - Otto Dix offers a decadent depiction of social life with dancing, cabaret and music. The vibrant colours in his 1928 painting of Weimar Germany, 'Os Noctivagos', shows dancers rotating their legs as in the Charleston. Each figure is depicted with a dance style emphasizing their body type in a caricatured way.
    - Rudolf Laban was himself involved in the Dada cabaret, and this early style of modern dance is captured in photographs from this period. See *Rudolf Laban: An Extraordinary Life* (Valerie Preston-Dunlop, London, 2008).
- Music:
    - Ragtime: Scott Joplin's piano music can be used to improvise dances with isolated body parts, and also inspire dramatic scenarios that can be staged in a silent movie style, requiring characters to hold onto their specific movement style while interacting with others, following a simple story line.
    - Dance bands specializing in music of the 1920s, such as The Passadena Roof Orchestra, have recorded vaudeville numbers that were popularized as social dances. Create your own dance craze routines to these show-stopping numbers, such as *The Varsity Drag*.

CONCLUSION:
THE FINAL BOW

Dance Foundations

Throughout the twentieth century, Rudolf Laban was involved with those searching for a new form a dance that was modern and expressed the experiences of the present day world. In his own explorations, Laban considered a possible syllabus for training actors, returning to ancient philosophical and mystical concepts alongside scientific research into movement. The study of dances from history was a significant part of this work, also contributing in some way to his creation of a comprehensive notation system to record movement of the human body. Laban posed the question of the value of considering history with dance, and his ideas can be summarized in his own words:

> Do the remnants of the historical art of dancing offer a sufficient foundation on which to build the new dance tuition in school, or do we need, in our complex modern civilisation, a new approach to the problem?
>   The answer is, I think, that we must look around us and compare the conditions of life in our time with those of the days in which the traditional dance forms originated.
>   (Rudolf Laban, 'Introduction', *Modern Educational Dance*, London, 1963)

I invite you, as a dancing actor, to make connections between the past and the present, and take this into the future.

Bringing it all Together

The function of dance as a dramatic art includes a contribution to narrative, character, concepts and theme. It is involved in the dynamic relationship between all these elements. Dance in a dramatic context may be the point where abstract ideas and physical expression become joined. For this reason, this book has considered a way of analyzing movement (Laban Dance) and a way of taking this to a level of performance which can stand alone (Show Dance). Evidence of moments in the past when people danced in a particular way to communicate their emotional feelings can fuel your imagination as an actor as you step back in time (Historical Dance) and inspire you to work creatively with the material while sharing these sensations with others as a new collaborative experience (Expressive Dance).

Only One Take

Please don't consider this book a definitive dance manual to allow you to perform the most perfect version of an historical dance. The Dance Reconstruction examples should be considered as only one way of performing the material. Other physical decisions may be made from the historical evidence that is available, with many different interpretations and inspirations. Most importantly, there will be gaps that always have to be filled by thinking actors, who must consider what feels right to them, having engaged with the many approaches and connected to their own ideas from their own research. They will convey their own intentions in communicating their character, interacting with the ensemble and adhering to the theatrical style chosen for the presentation. Even though historical dance may require the body to move in different 'hysterical' ways, don't forget that human beings created dance for human beings. Each dance form had a real social reason for existing at the time it did, and when it was being danced it would have been considered in some way to be natural and normal by at least some, if not all, of the people living at the time. It is this believable essence that we are hoping to find by considering dance as part of the art of creating drama, and then we can communicate this essence in an immediate way in performance today.

Complementing the Curriculum

This approach complements a drama school curriculum that includes movement training to develop the physical skills of the moving body of the actor. This area of dance in particular connects to the actor's sense of historical context and sets out to extend the repertoire of styles that can be physically presented in performance. If as an actor you also know some of the concepts that governed historical belief systems, then you can start believing in the material as being real for your character. One main question that should always be asked in practice is how does the dance connect both to the individual character and the overall drama being presented?

Moving Words

Although this book has presented written descriptions and verbal definitions, I am not advocating the need for a confined dance vocabulary, as the discovery of each movement quality should encourage you to use your own words that have meaning for the actual place where the dance is to be performed and the person doing the dance. Language develops over time, as styles change and new ways of communicating come into being. It is my hope that the suggestions of different ways of approaching the dimension of dance will help you actively engage with the dance material from previous historical periods and inspire you to make dynamic choices for how to present dance in the drama, in the moment of now.

Inspirations from Past Experience and Current Situations

I have taken much inspiration from dancing masters and choreographers from the past who have expressed their thoughts and recorded their approaches in many different ways. Numerous teachers and practitioners have shared their understanding through classes, practical reconstructions and newly created choreographies. I continue to find great value myself in using movement to generate new dances for theatrical events and to create social events where dance can bring people together in a physical way. This book is a result of having explored my ideas with many students and having worked as a choreographer and director with many performers. Each time I begin working on a project with a new group of students or performers, I am fascinated by the feedback that each person gives and how everyone responds individually, sometimes finding what I myself have found before, but also discovering new ways to develop the same idea into practical dance. I would like to take this opportunity to thank all those teachers, colleagues, performers, students, family and friends who have been part of this process along the way, and continue to be my inspiration.

Personal Thanks

The final word of acknowledgement must go to those close friends who have offered their support during the time I was writing this book. Like nine angelic muses, they would not let me give up and gave their own words of wisdom to me at very vital moments: Jillie Frost, Christopher Huntley, Tamsin Stanley, Jo Jones, Jo Lynch, Penelope Boff, Fiona Johnston, Sam Taylor and my mother Mary. The book is now complete.

Closing Credits

The actual physical form of this book and video content would not have been possible without the collaboration between RADA and the Nonsuch Dancers, initiated by Director Ed Kemp's invitation to involve Nonsuch with the Big Dance London festival.

RADA (www.rada.ac.uk)

RADA includes dance and movement training in all the courses which I have been privileged to teach. These include short courses and workshops (Acting Shakespeare, European Greats, Musical Theatre, Youth Access, RADA Enterprises, Shakespeare Summer School, Young Actors Summer School), the Foundation Course in Acting (Dance History, Show Dance, Choreography), the BA (Hons) in Acting (Dance and Choreography in Productions), the MA Theatre Lab and MA Text and Performance (Laban Approach and Historical Dance) and the New York University/RADA TISCH programme (Dance in the Arts of Shakespeare).

Nonsuch History and Dance (www.nonsuchdance.co.uk)

Nonsuch is a charitable organization that uses dances from history 'to teach, to train and entertain'. Historical dance research and tuition occurs at annual summer courses, along with support from the Early Dance Circle, with dance instruction manuals with accompanying music being produced to supplement the repertoire of dances. The former artistic director of Nonsuch, Peggy Dixon (1921–2005), compiled nine volumes of published manuals, from the medieval period to the nineteenth century, supervising the creation of recorded music suitable for dance reconstruction. Special thanks must be given to Professor Nira Pullin of Wayne State University, who worked as a guest teacher on the summer courses and shared her own research and practical knowledge of Ragtime and the Charleston. The Dance Reconstructions required input from many students and colleagues who explored the manuscripts in the studio to find a practical realization of the material. The exploratory research and practical work continues, under the management of the Board of Trustees of the Nonsuch History and Dance charity.

The Nonsuch Dancers

The professional performing company established under my artistic direction now works regularly with organizations such as the British Museum, the Historic Royal Palaces, the National Trust, Pablo de Olavide University, the Sevilla Dance Conservatory and Birkbeck College, University of London, with many performances in historic locations throughout the UK. The company aims to find a dramatic way of presenting dance material from history that is educational and entertaining for a contemporary audience. *Dance in Art* lectures and demonstrations have been regularly presented by Siân Walters of the National Gallery, London. A combination of contemporary dance and Historical Dance was used to present a new dance theatre piece, *Rexesexus*, at the Place Theatre, London, with Fran Billington, Caryl Griffith, Sian Jones, Jennifer Robinson, Francesca Roche, Stephen Sparling, Benedict Smith and Tomos Young, with music directed by Andrew Charity and José Gandia. Following the European Association of Dance Historians conference, 'Fusion and Confusion', in Sevilla, organized by Penelope Boff in Carmona, the Nonsuch Dancers have been involved in the ongoing site-specific performance project based on the dance play *The Dance of the Deadly Sins* by Diego Sanchez de Badajoz, published in Sevilla 1554, initially researched by David Sánchez Cano in Madrid.

The Nonsuch dancers who took part in the Dance Reconstructions were, in order of appearance:

Tomos Young

Having been raised and educated in France, Tomos studied in the UK at Bird College, receiving a BA (Hons) in dance and theatre before joining LABAN as part of the postgraduate Transitions company. Alongside Nonsuch, he has worked internationally in musical theatre and contemporary dance theatre, with companies such as Interdigitalis, Kari Hooas Productions and StopGap, and develops his own choreography with TYDC (Tomos Young Dance Company). Tomos has worked as a principal dancer and actor on a number of projects at the Haugesund Teater in Norway, choreographed by Darren Royston, with Artistic Director Birgit Amalie Nilssen.

Francesca Perissinotto Delle Roche

Francesca trained at the BRIT School, before studying Musical Theatre at Bird College, receiving a first-class BA (Hons) degree. She works as a dancer and actress, appearing as Dora in *Steel Pier*, Jane in *Girlfriends*, Forest Witch in *Hansel and Gretel*, and in *The Gladiator Girls* and equestrian stunt shows at the NEC in Birmingham. She has also featured in *Strictly Come Historical Dancing* at the Royal Shakespeare Company, Stratford, as well as dancing for *The Mighty Boosh* for Baby Cow Productions. Francesca worked as assistant to Darren Royston in the GEMS International Schools programme in Dubai, and in Spain at the Pablo Olavide University and Sevilla Dance Conservatory.

Benedict Smith

Benedict is a graduate of the RADA Foundation in Acting course. He began performing professionally at the age of five, being directed by Stephen Daldry in *An Inspector Calls* in the West End. He played the urchin role of Gavroche in *Les Miserables* at the Palace Theatre, London, and was in the original cast of *Chitty Chitty Bang Bang* at the Palladium. Benedict also played the main role of Harvey Johnson in Disney's *Life Bites* for two series, a children's sitcom that had a viewing figure of around two million. In addition to acting in film, TV and theatre, he continues to incorporate his dance skills in live performance, appearing in the *Jesus Christ Superstar* UK arena tour.

Faye Maughan

Faye trained at the London Studio Centre, graduating with a BA (Hons) in Theatre Dance, and received an MA in Acting from the Birmingham School of Acting. She was dance captain for the national tour of *One Night in Vegas* and has performed as a solo singer in a music hall tribute with the Players' Theatre Company, a dancer on cruise ships and in circus in South America. She holds a BASSC certificate in stage combat, displaying her fighting skills at the Globe Theatre and in the feature film *John Carter*. Other film work includes Karen in *All Fried Up* and Sarah in *Letters from the Front*. Theatre work includes playing Helena in an open-air production of *A Midsummer Night's Dream*.

Daniel Wilby

Daniel trained on the RADA Foundation Course in Acting, and works as an actor and musician. He performed as Sinjin in *Jane Eyre* with the Crescent Theatre Company, as Benny in *Bridges and Balloons* with the Imaginary Friends Theatre Company, an original piece at the Rag Factory on Brick Lane, and as The Watch in Shakespeare's *Much Ado About Nothing* at Ludlow Castle. Dan joined the Nonsuch Dancers to perform at Hampton Court Palace, and with the National Gallery in London, performing as an actor and dancer in *Leonardo da Vinci, Court Painter in Milan*.

Jo Bartlett

Jo graduated with a Diploma in Dramatic Art and a Licentiateship of the Royal Academy of Music in Speech and Drama, returning to Middlesex University to teach Movement for Actors before completing the RADA Acting Shakespeare course. Jo trained in Historical Dance with Nonsuch, leading performances at the British Museum, Hampton Court Palace and Kenwood House. Other collaborations include those with BBC Radio 3, Channel Four (the *5 O'clock Show*), Hever Castle, Rochester Cathedral and the Royal Shakespeare Company. Jo has taught dance on the Shakespeare in Performance at RADA, choreographing productions and teaching dance on the Foundation Course in Acting.

Nonsuch: Costume

Hanna Randall

The historical costuming of the filmed dances was supervised by Hanna Randall while a student on the RADA Theatre Costume course. Hanna made reconstructions of historical costumes for the Leonardo da Vinci exhibition presentation at the National Gallery, and full Elizabethan costumes for the *Rexesexus: Tudor Dirty Dancing* performance that formed part of the Resolution! Festival at the Place Theatre in London. Since graduating from RADA, Hanna has been based in New Zealand. Her credits include *The World of Wearable Art* (New Zealand), *Madame Butterfly* (New Zealand Opera), *The Glass Menagerie* (Auckland Theatre Company), *I am Wolf* (The Place Theatre, London) and *Mary Stuarda* (New York City Metropolitan Opera).

Nonsuch: Filming

Oliver Goater

Oliver worked as a freelance editor and motion graphics designer in London, before returning to New Zealand to study for a BA in Visual Effects and 3D animation.

Nonsuch: Editing

Jed Staton

Jed works at RADA as part of RADA Enterprises.

Nonsuch: Dance Direction

Darren Royston

My first memory of seeing dramatic dance was as a young boy during the school holidays, sitting crossed-legged under the director's table in a rehearsal of the Huddersfield Light Opera Society. The director was my grandfather, Norman Royston, who had spent many hours on the amateur stage, performing as a leading man. Soon after this, I played the part of the Ogre in the primary school musical, wearing a papier-mâché mask with a large club made by my dad, and appeared as Cinderella's Mother at the cub-scouts, wearing my mum's shawl and grandma's wig. My professional debut as a dancing-actor was as an urchin in Lionel Bart's *Oliver!* at the Harrogate Theatre, and this experience made me dedicate my life to dramatic performance.

Music, dance and drama classes in Harrogate at St Aidan's High School and the Katrina Hughes School of Theatre Art gave me practical techniques, including piano, viola, singing, speech and drama, tap, jazz and ballet. All these skills were useful when I joined the National Youth Theatre, where I met choreographers Imogen Claire and David Toguri, and I began to understand how choreography could be created as part of the drama. While studying English Literature at Queens' College, Cambridge, I focused on the development of drama through history, specializing in Shakespeare in Performance and the dance forms used in Shakespeare's plays, playing characters including Romeo and Benedict and directing *Much Ado About Nothing*. My dissertation on the Victorian representation of history in Gilbert and Sullivan operas connected to a large-scale production of *Patience* that I directed and choreographed as the first student performance at the Cambridge Corn Exchange, performed in the presence of HRH Prince Philip, the Duke of Edinburgh. I also spent too many hours involved in student drama at the ADC theatre, choreographing comedy with the Footlights (including now popular comic celebrities such as Sacha Baron-Cohen, David Mitchell and Robert Webb). I found I had a particular skill working with non-dancers, taking the role of choreographer and movement director for plays, musicals, operas and even a fashion show with Yasmin Le Bon, directed by Claudia Winkleman.

One day, in the Cambridge University library, I came across a book entitled *The Mastery of Movement for the Stage* written by Rudolf Von Laban. I was fascinated by the ideas in this book, and this led me to the Laban Centre in London where, under the direction of Marion North, I undertook postgraduate research in dance studies to Masters level with distinction. I received instruction from other practitioners who had also worked directly with Rudolf Laban, including Valerie Preston-Dunlop, Geraldine Stephenson, Jean Newlove, Warren Lamb, and disciples who had developed Laban's ideas further at the Laban Centre for Movement and Dance (LABAN) and with the Laban Guild for Movement and Dance, including Jean Jarell and Anna Carlisle. Receiving the Lisa Ullmann Scholarship, I undertook research into the Icelandic *sagna dans*, assisting Sigriður Valgeirsdottir in Reykjavik. My research into the role of dance in opera and classical theatre gave me work experience with choreographers at the English National Opera and Royal Shakespeare Company, including Stuart Hopps, Michael Keegan-Dolan, Terry John Bates, Nicola Bowie, Gillian Lynne, Sue Lefton and Jane Gibson, and I was fortunate to be an assistant on a number of projects.

I trained in historical dance in London with the Imperial Society for Teachers of Dancing (ISTD) at the Royal Academy of Dance (RAD) and in workshops with the Dolmetsch Historical Dance Society (DHDS) and the Early Dance Circle (EDC). I also worked with Madeleine Inglehearn at the Guildhall School for Music and Drama (GSMD) before becoming an assistant to Peggy Dixon, combining my academic research into dance history with practical teaching and performing with Nonsuch. Receiving the Bonnie Bird Choreography Award launched my freelance career as a choreographer in plays, musical theatre and opera, working with such companies as the English Touring Theatre, the European Chamber Opera, the Lord Chamberlain's Men, Battersea Arts Centre, the Royal National Theatre, the Old Vic Theatre, the Royal Shakespeare Theatre and at the Royal Opera House. As a teacher at RADA, I now bring these many different areas together frequently, and I encourage my students to journey into the unknown of the moment, knowing that they carry with them a wealth of knowledge and experience that can combine with their own creative energy and imagination. I hope that when you put this book down you will experience the ideas of dramatic dance in a physical way that means something to you as an individual artist, making your own expressive choices that connect to your own personal thoughts.

Taking Leave: The Final Bow

I have written this book for all those who make a commitment to using the physical body as the medium for expression in performance and continue to celebrate the Dionysian power of dance as one of the dramatic arts.

FURTHER STUDY

Historical Dance Approach

Dance Research Societies offer practical workshops and publications related to current work in historical dance research.

The National Resource Centre for Historical Dance (c/o The Early Dance Circle)

The Early Dance Circle: www.earlydancecircle.co.uk

The European Association of Dance Historians: http://www.eadh.com

The Dolmetsch Historical Dance Society: www.dhds.org.uk

The Annual Oxford Dance Symposium: www.new.ox.ac.uk/annual-oxford-dance-symposium

The Society for Dance Research: www.sdr-uk.org

The Society for Dance History Scholars: https://sdhs.org/

The International Council for Dance, UNESCO: www.cid-portal.org/

Acadanza Historica Sevilla: www.acadanza.com

Particularly Relevant to this book:

National Resource Centre for Historical Dance, *The Early Dance Circle: Primary Dance Sources Annotated Bibliography.* The information sheet Dance Through History details dance manuals and secondary sources. See www.earlydancecircle.co.uk.

Articles by Darren Royston include:

Proceedings of the Early Dance Conference, *Dance and Society*, edited by Barbara Segal & Bill Tuck, Farnham Castle, Surrey, 2012. Including 'Out of this World: Did Elizabethan court society really want to dance with the planets?' by Darren Royston.

Proceedings of the Sixth Dolmetsch Historical Dance Society Conference, *The Minuet in Time and Space,* 1997. Including 'Rudolf Laban's Minuet in Choreographie (1926)' by Jeffrey Scott Longstaff, Andrea Treu and Darren Royston.

Publications

Dixon, Peggy, *Nonsuch History and Dance: Dances from the Courts of Europe,* London: Nonsuch History and Dance, 1986/1998. Nine volumes of dance manuals and music reconstructions from the medieval period to the nineteenth century. See www.nonsuchdance.co.uk.

Hilton, Wendy, *Dance of Court and Theatre: French Noble Style, 1690–1725,* London: Pendragon Press, 1981.

Holme, Bryan, *Princely Feasts and Festivals, Five Centuries of Pageantry and Spectacle,* London: Thames and Hudson, 1988.

Inglehearn, Madeleine, *The Minuet in the Late Eighteenth Century,* including a reprint of S. J. Gardiner's A Dancing Master's Instruction Book of 1786, London: Madeleine Inglehearn, 1997.

Laver, James, *A Concise History of Costume,* London: Thames and Hudson, 1969.

McGowan, Margaret M., *Dance in the Renaissance: European Fashion, French Obsession,* New Haven, CT: Yale University Press, 2008.

Mullally, Robert, *The Carole: A Study of a Medieval Dance,* Surrey: Ashgate, 2011.

Nevile, Jennifer (ed.), *Dance, Spectacle and the Body Politick, 1250–1750,* Bloomington, IN: Indiana University Press, 2008.

Rogers, Ellis A., *The Quadrille. A Practical Guide to its Origin, Development and Performance,* Orpington, 2003.

Sharp, Cecil J. and Oppé, A. P., *The Dance: An Historical Survey of Dancing in Europe,* London: E.P. Publishing,1972. Includes black and white reproductions of dance depicted in art from each historical period.

Sparti, Barbara (ed.), *Guglielmo Ebreo of Pesaro: On the Practice or Art of Dancing,* Oxford: Clarendon Press, 1993. Includes the chapter 'Dancing in Fifteenth-Century Italian Society'.

Laban Dance Approach

Laban Guild for Movement and Dance promotes publications, courses, conferences and other events related to the approach to dance and movement initiated by Rudolf Laban. www.labanguild.org.uk.

Reference material is published in the journal *Movement, Dance and Drama*.

The Drama Representative on the Council is Darren Royston.

Publications

Guest, Ann Hutchinson, *Dance Notation, The Process of Recording Movement on Paper,* London: Dance Books,1984.

Laban, Rudolf, *Modern Educational Dance*, London: MacDonald, 1948.

—The Mastery of Movement on the Stage, revised by Lisa Ullmann, London: Northcote House,1950.

—Choreutics, annotated and edited by Lisa Ullmann, London: MacDonald and Evans, 1966.

Lamb, Warren and Watson, Elizabeth, *Body Code, The Meaning in Movement*, London: Routledge & Kegan Paul,1979.

McCaw, Dick, *The Laban Sourcebook*, London: Routledge, 2011.

Newlove, Jean, *Laban for Actors and Dancers*: Putting Laban's Movement into Theory, London: Nick Hern Books, 1993.

Newlove, Jean and Dalby, John, *Laban for All,* London: Nick Hern Books, 1994.

North, Marion, *Personality Assessment Through Movement,* London: Northcote, 1972. Appendix includes a glossary of terms and concepts of the Laban approach to movement study.

Preston-Dunlop, Valerie, *Rudolf Laban: An Extraordinary Life,* London: Dance Books, 2008.

History Guide Books

Overview

Nagler, A. M., *A Source Book in Theatrical History,* New York, 1952. Lists primary material chronologically.

Tierney, Tom, *Historic Costume From the Renaissance through the Nineteenth Century,* Mineola, NY: Dover Publications, 2004.

Pitkin Guides:

Provide a brief overview, visual images, quotations and historical timelines.

Brimacombe, Peter, *The Elizabethans*.

Brimacombe, Peter, *Life in Tudor England*.

Hayward, Edward, *Upstairs and Downstairs*.

St John Palmer, Michael,

—The Civil War 1642–51.

—Life in Georgian Britain.

—Life in Victorian Britain.

—*The War of the Roses.*
—*The World of Dickens.*
Williams, Brenda, *Victorian Britain.*
Williams, Brenda and Williams, Brian, *Kings and Queens.*
Willoughby, Rupert, *Life in Medieval England 1066–1485.*

Thames and Hudson Guides:
Fitzroy, Charles, *Renaissance Florence on Five Florins a Day,* London: Thames and Hudson, 2008.
Matyszak, Philip, *Ancient Athens on Five Drachmas a Day,* London: Thames and Hudson, 2008.
Tames, Richard, *Shakespeare's London on Five Groats a Day,* London: Thames and Hudson, 2008.

LIST OF ONLINE NONSUCH DANCE RECONSTRUCTIONS

01 French Basse Dance; La Dame https://vimeo.com/78832714

02 Royal Estampie; La Quinte Estampie Real https://vimeo.com/78832715

03 Italian Bassadanza for 2; Alexandresca https://vimeo.com/78832716

04 Italian Bassadanza for 4; Pellegrina https://vimeo.com/78833749

05 Italian Ballo for 2; Rostibolly Gioioso https://vimeo.com/78832719

06 Italian Ballo for 4; Anello https://vimeo.com/78834075

07 New Almaine https://vimeo.com/78834181

08 La Volta https://vimeo.com/78834182

09 Italian Balletto; Torneo Amoroso https://vimeo.com/78834185

10 Washerwomen's Branle https://vimeo.com/78834186

11 Country Dance for 2 couples; Rufty Tufty https://vimeo.com/78834187

12 Country Dance for 3 couples; Shepherds' Holiday https://vimeo.com/78835324

13 Country Dance for 3 couples; Picking of Sticks https://vimeo.com/78835325

14 The Ballroom Minuet https://vimeo.com/78835327

15 Bourreé https://vimeo.com/78835328

16 Allemanding https://vimeo.com/78835329

17 Mazurka https://vimeo.com/78836934

18 Polka https://vimeo.com/78836935

19 Charleston https://vimeo.com/78836936